LESSONS LEARNED FROM THE STARFISH

A TEACHER'S JOURNEY WITH CHILDREN OF POVERTY

MELANIE PARRISH ANDERSON

In partnership with Ghost Light Publishing

This book is a memoir. The author has recreated events, locales and conversations from memory. In order to protect the privacy of those discussed, names of individuals and places may have been altered. Some identifying characteristics and details such as physical properties, occupations and places of residence may have also been changed.

Print ISBN: 1-943367-14-0
Print ISBN-13: 978-1-943367-14-6

Cover Starfish Illustration:
Sarah Houghton, student of Ms. Melanie
Cover Typography:
Brenna Miller, granddaughter of Ms. Melanie
Interior Starfish Illustration:
Adria Miller, granddaughter of Ms. Melanie

Cover Design: CallyAnn Hamilton
Formatting: L.C. Ireland

www.MelanieParrishAnderson.com

Lessons Learned from the STARFiSH

A Teacher's Journey with Children of Poverty

Melanie Parrish Anderson

DEDICATION

Thank you, Mommy, for your constant encouragement. And thanks to my sister, Allyson, and her girls L.C. and CallyAnn, for pushing me to finish this project. And thank you to Kevin for your constant support. A special thank you to my children, Kimberly and Jordan, who lived every wonderful and heart-breaking story with me.

FOREWORD

ANN LEWIS, ELEMENTARY SCHOOL COUNSELOR

I was lucky enough to have the experience of student teaching with Melanie Anderson when I was pursuing my teaching degree. It was a magical experience watching her teach children. Her love, care and concern for each student was inspiring to watch. I went on to obtain a master's degree in counseling and was fortunate enough to work as a school counselor in the same school where Melanie teaches.

In all my years of counseling children in the elementary school setting, I have observed different teaching styles and educational theories. Melanie is a teacher that understands children and approaches teaching from the child's perspective and engages them in the learning process because she makes learning fun. Her students look forward to coming to class each day because they know their teacher will present the lesson for that day with enthusiasm for learning and with a fresh approach they will find interesting. She is a child centered teacher.

Melanie has positively impacted children through her love and commitment to education. As the school counselor, I have counseled many of the children that are in the stories found in this book.

I know their lives are better because they had Melanie as their teacher.

Melanie is always striving to be a better teacher. Melanie gives back by training many student teachers and evangelizes her noble idea that the children come first and learning is about engaging them to want to learn. Melanie is a master teacher.

In telling these stories, Melanie has opened a window into the struggle of teaching children and the incredible joy that comes from teaching when it works because the children choose to learn. You can learn a lot about life from the stories she tells of how these children courageously navigate their lives filled with challenges and opportunities to learn and grow. She tells the stories in the way she teaches – with energy, excitement, and enthusiasm. Her stories will engage you and consequently you will be convinced learning can be fun and life can be fun!

Ann Lewis, LPC
Elementary School Counselor

PREFACE

The first time I read *The Star Thrower* by Loren Eiseley, I was touched by the wisdom of the little boy who was picking up the starfish and throwing them back into the ocean. When questioned what he was doing by an old man walking along the beach, the boy replied, "The tide stranded them. If I don't throw them in the water before the sun comes up, they'll die."

To which the old man answered, "Surely, you realize that there are miles of beach and thousands of starfish. You'll never throw them all back — there are too many. You can't possibly make a difference."

I was so impressed by the boy's reply when, as he picked up another starfish and threw it back into the ocean, he politely responded, "Well, it makes a difference to this one!"

It makes a difference to this one became a powerful lesson to me, especially because it came from a child. It would set a course for my life, even though, at the time, I didn't realize the remarkable influence.

THE HARD KNOCKS OF TEACHING

In 2012, Idaho's Superintendent of Education followed through on his proposal of a "Pay-for-Performance" initiative that had passed through the legislature. I do agree that, on the surface, the idea was a great one, as I feel that teachers are the most overworked and underpaid professionals in America. The bonuses went out to all the schools that could show significant improvement in the scholastic achievement of students between the fourth and fifth grades. The same students were tested in fourth grade and again in fifth grade to show how much they had grown. The whole school was judged on one test on one day of fourth grade against another test the students took on one day in fifth grade. Believe me, we all hoped and prayed that those were good days.

At our school, they weren't good days.

One of our biggest issues was the number of transients we had at our school. Generally speaking, poverty-stricken families tend to move around a lot as places to live become available or as they get evicted again and again. In fact, only 61 percent of our fourth graders returned to be tested in fifth grade.

At the time, I taught second grade, and I was very excited about the pay-for- performance idea, as I had raised my second graders' scores from 38-percent proficiency on the fall I.R.I. to 95-percent proficiency in the spring. The Idaho Reading Inventory is a standardized test that only accounts for reading speed. It does not test fluency or comprehension. This means that 24 out of 25 of my students were reading at least 92 words per minute. Reading at 92 words per minute is the second grade standard for a student at grade level. It was my best year ever. My team and I had worked very hard to help these kids, and we were quite pleased to think we might be appreciated for it.

We were devastated to find out that, not only were we not going to receive the bonus, but that we were the only elementary school in the whole district that didn't. I was shocked, as my numbers were some of the best in the city.

Incidentally, I teach at a low-income, high-poverty school. More than 80 percent of the students at my school live below the poverty line and are eligible for free and reduced lunch, just like all of the schools who didn't receive the pay-for-performance bonuses were.

So does that mean the teachers are terrible, or does that mean that the students' lives are so tough that they spend a lot of time worrying about where they are going to sleep? Or when they were going to eat again. Or how their parents were going to pay the rent. Or when their dad was going to be getting out of jail. Or if someone was going to be home when they arrived home from school. The list goes on and on.

They seemed to worry more about life than they did about reading or math or school. I know my kids cared about learning, but when it came to testing, perhaps the comparatively lower scores of these impoverished students had less to do with their teacher's underperformance than it did with their disproportionate exposure to life's biggest challenges.

Not receiving the pay-for-performance bonuses was so disheartening and embarrassing for our school and its remarkable teachers, principal, and amazing staff. Many of my friends and family asked me why I worked so hard in a profession full of a hierarchy that didn't seem to care about how hard we worked at all. It was not unusual for me to put in a 60-hour work week correcting papers, writing individualized learning plans for each of my students, making a scrapbook, reading my students' journals, writing letters to their parents, or writing lesson plans. High school teachers usually have a one-hour preparation period per day, which enables them to complete this stuff at school, but elementary teachers only have one 30-minute prep period per week. Other than our 35-minute lunch, we are with the kids all day every day. We must put in time outside of school to be successful.

By the way, second graders really like your attention and are very unhappy if you choose to correct papers while they feel you should be paying attention to them.

Teaching is a very demanding job, but I love it.

After the embarrassment of the pay-for-performance debacle, I really had to reassess my career choice. Was it all worth it? I worked so hard and cared so deeply about these kids.

The story of the starfish on the beach came back to my mind. I pictured that little boy picking up each struggling starfish lying on the sand and throwing it back into the ocean to save its life. I questioned, *Is it worth taking the time to save the starfish? Does it really make a difference? There are thousands and thousands of starfish struggling to survive along the beach. I can't save them all. There are thousands and thousands of children in need who want to be taught and cared for and saved. Does what I do really matter? I can only save 25 starfish per year, and sometimes, I can't even save all of those.*

But I know, with all my heart, that I do my best.

Do I make even a *little* difference in the lives of any of these children? An overwhelmingly powerful memory came back to my mind of that little boy on that beach holding that precious starfish, saying, "It makes a difference to this one!"

That was my answer. Maybe the ones I can save do matter. That is why I will keep teaching — that is why I chose the name of this book.

I have truly learned so many, many lessons from the starfish.

LEARNING TO TEACH

When I was a preteen, my parents decided we were going to have a family gathering called Family Home Evening every single Monday night. The leaders of my church suggested setting time aside weekly to help families bond and promote scripture study. Being a preteen, I thought the idea was ridiculous and pouted and stomped around and complained under my breath (and occasionally over my breath) about how silly it was to put me through this kind of torture. But I lost the fight and had to endure this meeting every Monday night.

My parents and all five of us kids (my brother Mark was born two years later) would gather in the living room. My mom always made us a yummy dinner beforehand, and we had a delicious dessert after the meeting. Nothing got in the way of Family Home Evening. We couldn't take phone calls, have friends over, or have any communication with the outside world. It was family time and that was it. Blah, blah, blah!

At first, I thought it was dorky because my little sisters and brother were annoying. I, of course, was so much cooler than them and often thought, "I don't need family home evening. It's for losers."

Apparently, my parents didn't care much about my feelings because, every Monday night, I was there with the other dorks in my family.

Considering my ornery attitude, this will come as no shock, but I hated — *hated* — practicing the piano despite my parents having put out good hard-earned money for lessons. My precious time was much better spent listening to the Osmonds or David Cassidy or any other of the teen heartthrobs of the day.

One thing my dad decided to do, which was brilliant, was to pay me $1.00 per hymn that I could practice on the piano and play well enough for our family to sing at Family Home Evening. I was thrilled about the money and tried to have a new hymn each week. It also helped me a lot when I figured out that I was a not-so-horrible piano player. I hated to practice, but if there was money involved, it changed the game.

I figured out that I could buy four *Tiger Beat* magazines per month for playing dumb songs on the piano. Brilliant, I say! Brilliant!

Each week, my mom or dad would prepare lessons based around scriptures or life lessons they felt we needed to learn. Both of my parents were great teachers and made the lessons very interesting. Even though I was pouting and complaining most of the time, I believe some of the things they taught actually had sunk in.

I started to notice that my mom would add visual aids into her lessons and that my dad would utilize object lessons. For example, my dad would take a pitcher of water, which represented a person, and fill it with water — the water being a representation of our souls. Then, he would add a few drops of food coloring to the water, which represented the sins we commit. Lastly, he would add bleach to the water, turning the now-colored water back to its original hue. He would then explain how repentance worked and that, just like the bleach did the water, it purifies our souls. My parents would find pictures and games that would help teach us the lesson we were learning. This made learning a lot more fun. I wasn't particularly into learning and still thought the whole thing was a waste of my time, except for the money I was earning.

After about six months, my dad said it was my turn to give the lesson. Of course, I asked how much he was going to pay me for that. He just smiled and said, "That's just being part of the family."

There was a lesson manual, and it even came with stuff for a flannel board story about Moses. Even though I didn't want anyone to know how excited I was, I colored all the pieces and cut them out and attached them to flannel material so they would adhere to the flannel board. (Flannel's what we used before Velcro was invented.) I believe I complained the whole week about it, but really, I was thrilled when Monday finally came.

I told the story of Moses' mom and how she had to put her tiny baby in a basket and put him in the river and send him away so the bad king wouldn't kill him. My story was brilliant because I added voices and made it a little scary and had worked extra hard on my coloring. My whole family sat there, riveted by my lesson. I couldn't believe it. Even my little sisters were paying attention. It was like magic.

At the time, my little brother Jonathan was just a baby, and I took him and held him in my arms and asked my family if they could imagine what it would be like if we were told to take our little brother and put him in a basket and send him down the river to save his life. I started to cry because I loved him so much. I passed out little baskets to each member of my family. Each basket held a baby that I had colored. I told them that God only asks us to do what we are strong enough to do even though it may be really, really hard.

After the lesson was over and we were on to the amazing dessert my mom had made, my dad came and put his arm on my shoulder and said "Melanie, I think you're a natural teacher. You made a good lesson great. You even taught the little children. I am so proud of you and the work you put in. I love that you taught them how they learn best."

He hugged me, which, at the time, I didn't think was cool, but I pretended to be okay with it, and then he walked away. I heard him say to my mom, "Doreen, I think she is going to grow up to be a teacher. She has a gift."

I have never forgotten that and have wondered all through my career if that was a foreshadowing of the road my life was to take, or if he really knew something I didn't. I was only 10 at the time, but I think I really learned the power that teaching can have!

Many more lessons followed with many more flannel board stories and many more crazy voices and pictures and object lessons, which helped me realize how much I loved teaching. The dreaded Family Home Evening was actually where I became a teacher!

PART I

TEACHING KINDERGARTEN AND TITLE ONE MATH

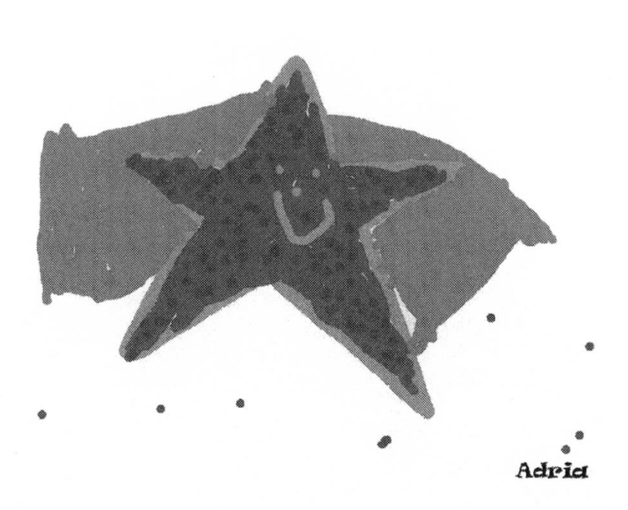

1

PETER

My first year of teaching was crazy busy. I had been offered a part-time job at one of the schools where I had student-taught, but the other school put two part-time jobs together so I could work full time, and they offered that to me. I took it.

Oh my goodness. It was insane.

My job included teaching 25 kindergarteners every morning from 8:25 to 11:45 and then teaching math to 30 third, fourth, and fifth graders. The preparation time was nuts. I would spend Saturdays preparing for kindergarten and Sundays preparing for math classes. I have never been so busy in my life. My own kids really suffered through this time. They practically became orphans.

Kindergarten was going fairly well. I was outnumbered 24 to 1, but I loved each one of my students. In those days, a lot of effort was put into teaching children through play. It's the Montessori Method of learning. I loved it and was amazed at the interesting and intriguing things the kids figured out at their own pace. I love learning that way, and so did the kids.

Fast forward to Halloween Day when into our happy little learning world came Hurricane Peter. I have heard about children like him, but I had never actually met one. I was pretty sure he had been raised by wolves or apes in a far-off jungle of Africa somewhere. He had no language. He would grunt or scream. He was in constant motion. He would continually jump up and down, and if he didn't get his way, he turned into a wild animal. He literally acted like a wild monkey having a temper tantrum. We were all dumbfounded.

We had been hit by earthquake Peter, and he registered at least 7.5 on the Richter Scale.

Note to all parents out there: If you're raising a wild animal in your home and are planning to enroll them in school late, do not start them on Halloween. Ever. Do not — I mean it. It will be a disaster for all concerned.

Peter was a tiny little thing but packed a powerful wallop. At first, I thought he was out of control because it was Halloween. I thought for sure he would calm down by the following Monday. I was terribly wrong. I found out from the social worker that he and his mother lived in some refrigerator boxes behind Albertsons.

Peter had had no social skills at all (no kidding) and hadn't interacted with other people, especially children. He had never seen a book or a classroom or a pencil or a teacher. The social worker was trying to get help for them because it gets cold in Idaho in October, and the only way she could get assistance for them is if they put him in school.

The kids and I spent a few days in shock with our mouths hanging open and watched as the little Tazmanian Devil destroyed everything in his wake. One of my colleagues soon pointed out that I was actually getting paid to teach and that I should probably figure out how to take control back of my classroom. I assured her that while I had really learned a lot about many many things and had been trained well by the Idaho State University Department of Education, I had never ever been taught how to handle the current anarchy going on in my classroom.

So while I managed the other 24 kindergarteners, I studied Peter. He was fascinating. He was in constant motion. Some part of his body was always moving. He didn't speak words but would point and yell or grunt and groan. During snack time, he would throw his food and napkin on the floor. At first, I would pick it up for him, and he would eventually eat it. But slowly, I stopped picking up his food for him, and he would have to go get it himself. Then, eventually, when he threw it, I would take it away altogether. Pretty soon, he stopped throwing it at all. I taught him to say "please" and "thank you" in sign language, and that helped a lot. He slowly — *very* slowly — learned how to act by watching the other kids — once he noticed that there were other kids.

One really big lesson I learned that first year was how empathetic and caring children can be. One day, while the social worker fought with Peter to take him to get his hearing checked, I had a meeting with my class. I asked them what they thought about Peter and if it was hard for them to learn with him in our class. I was expecting the kids to complain, but they didn't.

One little girl said, "I wish I knew how to help him. He might be very smart, you know."

Another one asked, "Do you think if I helped him he would stop knocking down all of my building blocks?"

And still another one asked, "Why do you think he is so angry? Do you think someone is mean to him?"

I was completely dumbfounded. The kids wanted to help him and were learning to care about him.

We made a plan together. Each day, one of the kids would be Peter's "Power Pal." (They came up with that name so they could show him he could have "good power" instead of "bad power.") They would sit by him during snack time and play next to him during learning time so that he could learn how to have manners. They taught him sign language for "friend" and "help you." It was a long, slow process, but the kids never gave up.

Pretty soon, he would watch what the other kids were doing until they invited him to play with them. I was amazed because, before that, he would destroy everything they were doing.

Miracles started to happen every day.

His speech was still nearly unintelligible until one day when a little girl ran up to me so excited. I thought she was going to wet her pants. She screamed, "Teacher, Peter said 'Pwease, fweind' for me to share a toy with him! He usually just grabs it, but I taught him to share." She squealed.

It was a real breakthrough, and the kids cheered for him. I have never seen a bigger smile on a little face than I did on Peter's that day.

Peter came to school every day really dirty. I am pretty sure he had never brushed his teeth or washed his face or hair. His golden-brown hair flowed half over his shoulders and looked really nice when it was washed. We even found an adorable little dimple in his cheek when his chubby little face was clean. I bought him some clean clothes and socks, and the PTO bought him a coat. The kids told him he was handsome. He grunted at them but had a huge smile on his face.

One day we had "Teeth Brushing Day." I showed all of the kids the correct way to brush their teeth. Then I sent the boys into the bathroom to all brush their teeth together. They told me Peter's favorite part was spitting, but they had to show him to spit in the sink and not on the floor. Our janitor deserved a medal that year in more ways than one. I gave Peter a brand new Mickey Mouse toothbrush, and his "Power Pal" for that particular day would help him brush his teeth.

His Pal, if it was a boy, would help him put on clean clothes. I would take the dirty clothes home and wash them. One day, one of the boys came to me and asked, "Teacher, do you know that Peter doesn't have any underalls?"

I wasn't sure what that meant, so he explained, "You know, those panties you wear under your clothes. Well, actually girls wear panties and boys wear underalls. He doesn't have any of those."

We solved that problem the very next day. I asked the boys what kind I should get. They informed me that Batman was the best and then Peter would be as cool as they were. While it was a little more information than I needed, Peter was a "Batman bum" the very next day.

Then one day, right before Christmas, another hurricane hit our little classroom. It was called "The Mother." Have you ever seen the movie *The Rescuers*? You know the lady in that movie who kidnaps the little girl to make her dig for the diamond down in the well? She was copied right off of Peter's mother. I only met her once, but wowzers! She was a large and in-charge lady with a big boufant hairdo, bright red lips, a flowered muumuu, sharp, knarly fingernails, and an attitude that could freeze boiling water. She had me shakin' in my boots.

She was mad at Peter for some reason that day and sort of drop-kicked him into our classroom. We all stood there sort of taken aback — as if the Wicked Witch of the North had just dropped a house on us or something. She blew into our classroom and rushed back out with even more force. I kept thinking of Glenda when she said, "People come and go so quickly around here."

Anyways, Peter came into the classroom and collapsed on the floor, sobbing and throwing a tantrum. I got the kids back to work the best I could. Some of the kids asked me, "What was that? Was that his mother or something?"

I wasn't sure myself, but said I thought so. It was frightening.

Something changed that day when Peter cried himself to sleep on the floor. About an hour later, he started to stir. I went and sat by him and started to pat his back. When he finally woke up, I smiled at him and whispered, "I'm really glad you're here. I hope we can have a happy day."

Peter didn't like to be touched — ever — and everyone knew it. But for some reason, that day, I decided to live on the wild side, and I patted his back and stroked his hair. I was unsure and a little scared about how he would react. He lay there for a long time. It was the first time I had ever seen him hold still. Eventually, I took my hand away and asked him if he wanted a snack. He grunted something and reached over and grabbed my hand and put it back on his back, and he rubbed it up and down. I got the message! He moved closer and closer to me so I would rub his back.

Finally, one of the other kids came over and said to him, "Peter, guess what. I am your Power Pal today. Do you want to sit by me for snack?"

He actually smiled and went with her.

From that day on, during story time, Peter would come and sit with me and hold still while I read the story to all of the kids. He had learned to love books. He would take my hand and rub it on his back until I did so myself. If I had to turn the page, he would hold my hand until I put it back on his back. I was truly amazed at the power that a gentle touch had over him. After the story, however, he was back to full speed ahead.

Our other major — and I mean major — challenge was getting him to hold a pencil correctly. I tried to explain that it was a pencil, not a knife used to stab a paper to death, but apparently, stabbing the thing was much more interesting. I held his hand with a pencil in it over and over again, trying to keep him from stabbing me or others and trying to help him form letters — or anything vaguely resembling letters. We tried right-handed and left-handed. We tried every way possible that a person could hold a pencil.

I came up with an idea that I was pretty sure was brilliant: shaving cream! I put shaving cream in front of each of the students to help them practice their letters.

Who knew shaving cream could go so very very wrong?

While the other kids had a blast writing their names and spelling words, Peter chose to slap shaving cream all over everything and everyone. I had it in my hair, on my clothes, on my shoes, and in my nose, as did Peter. At first, I was crazy mad and very disappointed that it didn't work. One of the kids started to laugh and asked if I was going as Santa Claus today. Then I started to laugh, and then everyone started to laugh. Peter stopped and looked at all of us like *we* were the crazy ones. Then, for some unknown reason, he went back to his table and started to write in the shaving cream.

His Power Pal said "Great job, Peter. Do you want me to show you how to write your name?"

He wrote P-E-T in the shaving cream. Peter looked at it and tried to copy him. He had written a sad-looking P-E-X-X-X, but I think he actually figured out what we were trying to teach him. After that, he figured out that his pencil could make things that looked like what the other kids were writing. Huge breakthrough!

Each year, our class did a program right before spring break. I would teach the kids a few songs in sign language and some fun songs about animals. One of the songs I taught them was "Brown Bear, Brown Bear." I made a poster of each of the animals from the song and taped them to yardsticks. As each verse came along, a different animal would appear. When we got to the green frog, Peter went nuts. He ran over and grabbed it from the little girl whom I had assigned to hold it, and he literally turned into a frog — with the ribbet and the hopping and all. I asked the little girl if I could give her a different animal, and she said as long as it was the purple cat.

I gave her the purple cat, and all was well.

On the day of the performance, the parents crammed into my room and watched the program. The kids were awesome. Peter even kind of sang (or something close to it) through the whole show. When we got to the final song, "Brown Bear, Brown Bear," I thought he was going to burst with excitement. He was hopping up and down waiting for his turn to hold up the green frog. When it finally came, he was the hoppingest, happiest green frog you have ever seen. It was pure joy for him. I could not believe this was the same angry, wild child that had joined my class that long-passed Halloween Day.

Of course, Peter's mother didn't come to the performance. The parents took their kids home or out to lunch after the show, so it was just Peter and me for about 35 minutes while we waited for his bus. I started to clean up the room, and Peter slammed himself down on the floor like he was pouting. I went over and sat by him. I told him he did a great job today. He took my hand and put it on his back and lay his head in my lap. I told him how happy I was that he had joined my class and how amazed I was that he could write P-E-T on his papers now and how he could get himself dressed and brush his teeth and his hair and put his stuff away all by himself. I told him how proud I was of him.

Then, I will never forget it as long as I live, he sat up on his knees and put his hand on my cheek and said, "Lovb you teachorb," and went and got me a book to read to him. He lay back down on my lap and put my hand on his back, and I read to him until his bus came. My heart melted that day.

That was the last time I ever saw Peter. He didn't come back after spring break. The social worker said she thought that "The Mother" was running from the law. I looked everywhere for them. I looked behind Albertsons. I went to the homeless shelters, and I looked at the apartment they had given her. Everything was gone. Peter was gone. There was no sign of them.

I was heartbroken.

My students were heartbroken. We made him a book of their favorite memories, and they drew pictures of him for him. Many of the kids were really worried about him and what was going to happen with "The Mother." I couldn't answer any of their questions, but I did tell them how incredibly proud I was of them for how they treated that little boy and how much it helped my heart that they cared about him, too.

That little boy changed all of our hearts!

2

MENTOR/FRIEND

When I started college, I knew I wanted to be a teacher. I looked closely at the Early Childhood Education program because it had interesting classes about childhood brain and emotional development and the learning stages children go through, as well as lots of other information. But I was also intrigued by the Elementary Education Department because it offered classes in curriculum development, classroom management, and other subjects I was interested in. I just continued to take interesting classes in both areas. At the end of my fourth year, my advisor noticed that I had enough credits to graduate from both programs if I went one more semester and then student-taught.

On May 13, 1993 (one of the happiest days of my life), I graduated from our local university with a Bachelor of Science Degree in Elementary Education and a Bachelor of Arts Degree in Early Childhood Education. It seemed like I had set my sights very high, but it was truly the inability to make a decision that got me to both degrees. Fortunately, it did end up paying off, as I was the only graduate hired full time that year.

When it came time to student-teach, I was assigned an eight-week session in a kindergarten class and an eight-week session in a fourth-grade class. I learned so much from both of my cooperating teachers. In one setting, I learned exactly how I wanted to teach, and in the other setting, I learned how I would *never* teach. Both experiences were incredibly valuable.

My cooperating teacher in kindergarten was remarkable. You could tell she loved the kids and took their learning very personally. She worked tirelessly to figure out how each child learned and processed what they learned. She made learning so much fun that the kids didn't even realize they were working so hard to learn. I remember watching her teach and being mesmerized by her. I would answer her questions right along with the kids. I wanted to sing the songs and color the pictures and work with the math manipulatives and do all the things they did. I wanted to teach just like her and love and impact the kids as much as she did. You could tell she loved to teach.

She taught me one of the greatest lessons of my career. She was on the committee to hire the new kindergarten teacher and had put in a good word for me. Because of that, I was hired to teach, and I had her as my mentor.

She guided me through my first year. She would check on me every day and answer all my questions and listen to my many, many concerns. Every new teacher needs a good, patient mentor. She would make me laugh at how ridiculous so many of the things that happened were. She helped me learn to love teaching.

She watched me struggle with Peter and gave me remarkable advice on how to handle him and his wacky behavior. She was invaluable and even offered to take him into her class if I needed her to, but she believed in me and believed that I could do it. And because of that, I was determined to never give up on that kid. I was determined to save this one starfish. She taught me all kinds of real-world strategies you can't learn in college, even with two degrees.

I was devastated when Peter didn't come back to school after spring break. My mentor listened to me patiently as I fretted and stewed about what had happened to him. I looked for him for several weeks and worried and complained and missed him!

Finally, after about a month, I whined to her. "I don't know if I can handle this job. It's too emotionally draining and takes too much out of me. I get way too attached to the kids, and I'm devastated that Peter was taken away from me without my permission. I couldn't believe that, after all I had invested in him, 'The Mother' just stole him away from me!"

My kind mentor stoically listened to me for a long, long time. When I finally finished, she patiently asked, "Are you done yet?"

I was taken aback and intelligently said, "Huh?"

Very kindly and with much empathy and love, she calmly said, "Okay, stop! Do not ever make this job about you and what you can handle and what you get out of it and how it affects you. The fact of the matter is that you were the best thing that has ever happened to little Peter. He has never been cared for and taught the way you did him. You changed him, you loved him, and you were the best, most consistent thing in his life. Even if it was just for a short time, you made a difference for that little boy as you have for all the children in your class. Teachers who burn out make it about them. Teachers who love to teach make it about the kids whose lives they touch, and those teachers allow the kids' lives to touch them. Learn to love them and let them love you, and then let them go. They will always remember that their teacher cared about them!"

I appreciated that advice so much and have taken it into my heart. When I have children who are really tough or who have lives that are horrible, I remember those words: "It's not about you; it's about what you can do for them!"

I have hurt so much for the things that some of my kids (students: they will always be my kids, even when they are all grown up) have had to go through and by choices that have been made by the adults in their lives. The choices that the kid had no control over, but was affected by so much. I try to be a beacon for them, making sure that they know they are cared for and that they matter — that they have choices in the world that will make a difference in their lives and that will affect their future.

Thank you to my wonderful mentor for teaching me, for guiding me, for being my mentor, and especially for being my friend. I did get to teach with her for the next 18 years until she retired! I am truly grateful!

3

MICHAEL

During my student teaching, I met an adorable little tow-headed boy named Michael. Every day, he wore slacks, a white-collared shirt, dress shoes, and a tie to school. His hair was always combed, slicked down, and carefully parted on the side. He carried a miniature brief case, which he put his papers and books in every day and carried it to and from school. He seriously looked like a little businessman going to work.

Every morning, when he walked into class, he would walk up to me and politely say, "Good morning, student-teacher lady. It's nice to see you." Then he'd walk over to Mrs. E. and say, "Good morning, Mrs. E. I am happy to be here today, and I am ready to learn."

I was amazed by this little young man, who was only in kindergarten. One day, he was at my station and working very hard. I said to him casually, "Hey Michael, you always look so nice when you come to school. I was just wondering if you would tell me about that."

He thought about it for a minute and looked up at me with his big blue eyes and very seriously said, "You know, Teacher, school is serious business, and I am very serious about it. Actually, school is my work job!"

Shortly after this, I talked to Michael's mom about how professional he looked and acted every day. She chuckled and described their morning routine. "Oh Miss Melanie, you should see him and his father. They tie their ties and their shoes at the same time. They stand next to each other, looking in the mirror as they make sure their shirts are clean and pressed. They eat breakfast mirroring each other. Dad drinks his coffee, and Michael drinks his hot chocolate or juice at the very same time. It's adorable. They wipe their mouths on their napkins at the same time, ask me to be excused, put on their coats, and walk out the door together. They 'fist bump' and say 'Work hard and have a great day' at exactly the same time as they giggle and wave as they go their separate ways. It's like watching a grown man and his mini-me every day. It's the cutest thing I've ever seen."

I would have to agree with her.

4

ANDREA

Once I took over teaching the whole kindergarten classroom during my student-teaching experience, I found that it was so much work. It became a lot of fun when I watched the kids learn and grow with the curriculum I was presenting.

My cooperating teacher suggested that I ask the principal to observe me so that she could see what kind of teacher I was and how I interacted with the students. I invited her, and she was graciously willing to observe.

As part of the college education program, a monitor does an official observation. I was earning two degrees, so I had an advisor from both colleges, early childhood and elementary education. Including my cooperating teacher, there were four adults observing my lesson. They sat quietly in the back of the room, sitting at a table and scribbling down notes. In addition to the adults, there were 25 kindergarteners sitting on the floor listening to my lesson.

The lesson was about groups of people and animals. We had already talked about and drawn our parents and siblings, which was called a "family" of people. We were discussing different animal groups, including a school of fish, a flock of birds, a litter of cats, a herd of cows, a gaggle of geese, etc. The kids thought it was really funny that each group had its own name.

As we talked about the different groups, each child got to choose a picture of a different animal and identify it. The kids loved figuring out the species, then which animal family that particular animal would fit into. The kids were very intrigued and were participating. It was going great.

Unfortunately, I had not thought through all the family groups of animals. Joey came up and chose a picture of an octopus. He identified it and then said, "What would an octopus' family be called?"

As my brain quickly thought through all the possible answers, I noticed giggling coming from the adults in the back of the room. The adults were all snickering at the question and I soon figured out that the answer could very quickly become inappropriate. I tried like crazy to ignore them and go on with the lesson.

"Great job, Joey, and good question," I said nervously. "All right, you guys, what do you think an octopus' family could be called?"

There was a painfully long silence as all the adults in the room held our breaths, praying this would not become even more embarrassing for me than it already was. Slowly, a little girl named Andrea raised her hand. She was a beautiful little Chinese-American girl with bobbed, jet-black hair and dark black eyes. I pointed to her, and she cautiously said, "Teacher, I think a family of octopus is called ... an octo-crowd."

I wanted to hug her. The adults in the back of the room laughed and cheered and gave me a thumbs up. Thank goodness for Andrea and her higher-level thinking skills!

5

CHRISTOPHER D.

One year, I had eight students in my class with some form of the name Chris. We had Christopher D., Christopher L., Christopher P., Christopher W., Kris R., Kristen, Christy, and Krystal, five boys and three girls. It was crazy fun. I would often ask, "Will someone with some form of the name Chris please line up at the door?" or "If your name begins with a hard "C" sound, you may go to recess."

Toward the end of the year, I noticed some of the Christophers just started writing the alphabet letter for their last names on their papers because their name was so long. One of them asked me one day, "Teacher, why do so many other people haves the same name as me, and why does it haves to be so long?"

My answer seemed to satisfy him when I said, "Maybe because Christopher is such a *distinguished* name that a lot of parents wanted an important name for their child, too, like Christopher Columbus. He was a very important man, you know, like *you're* a very important young man!"

He seemed happy when he skipped away, but later, I heard him tell one of the other Christophers that their teacher thought their name was "ding-squished," but that he didn't know what that meant.

One of the fun units we did that year was a study of the oceans. Our back wall was covered with blue paper, and the children had constructed seaweed and "sea-grass," as the kids called it, because they didn't know how to make weeds and fish and sea creatures. They had made different sea animals to hang from the ceiling. Before we hung anything up, though, we had to figure out which of the animals could breathe air and which of the animals had gills. We hung the air-breathers from a string on the ceiling and pinned the gilled animals onto the blue-papered ocean.

Because I taught using a "whole-language" model, we had math games, science activities, stories, and social studies lessons based on the ocean, its place on earth, and the animals that lived in it. I brought in a real-life, dead octopus for the kids to touch and see how they could make it move in a huge tub of water. We had tons of shells, which they could sort and classify and make patterns. We also had sand in the sensory table that they could run their fingers through (and not throw).

One day, my principal came into my room at the end of school, looked around, talked to some of the kids, and then asked me to stop by his office after I had put the kids on the bus. He had had a phone call and was a little concerned.

Of course, I went into panic mode and searched my brain to try to figure out what the phone call could have been about. My principal was a delightful and fun-spirited man. He thought it was important to laugh every day and really enjoy life, especially if you were a teacher. I loved working for him because he created a happy, enjoyable, fun environment.

When I went into his office, he asked me to close the door and sit down. He was very serious, which was odd for him because he usually teased and laughed with me. He looked me right in the eye and asked, "Melanie, is it true that you told Christopher D. that he had the best testicles in the whole kindergarten class?"

I was dumbfounded. I honestly didn't know what to say. The principal didn't even crack a smile. I stuttered around for something to say and finally came out with, "I ... I ... I ... don't think I did. Why

... why ... why would I tell a child that? I ... I ... I ... I'm pretty sure I didn't um ... um ... um."

Finally, the principal smiled, laughed, and then explained, "I got a phone call from Christopher D.'s grandmother today because, apparently, last night, at a huge family dinner, Christopher stood up and announced to the whole family that his teacher told him that he had the best testicles in *all* of kindergarten, and they were wondering exactly how you knew that."

My mouth dropped open, and I was unable to complete a coherent sentence. He finally said, "You will be happy to know that I have already called the grandmother back and explained to her that indeed Christopher had the very best *tentacles* in the whole class. He showed me the octopus he had made, and he was the only one who patterned the colors when he glued on the tentacles. We had a really great laugh about it, and she wanted me to let you know how much he loves school and loves being in your class and that the whole family was amazed at how much he knew about oceans."

I was so relieved that it took me a minute to figure out that he had known the whole time about the octopus's tentacles, but that he had really enjoyed teasing me. In fact, the whole staff had a great laugh about it at the next faculty meeting and teased me about it for years.

6

TRENTON

One of the skills we work on in kindergarten is teaching the correct rules of writing. I made sure that the kids understood that when you write, you begin on the left side of the paper and travel right and start at the top and write to the bottom. It's the same way you read.

One year, I decided it would be a fun idea to demonstrate this skill to the kids every day by modeling the writing process and publishing a weekly newspaper called *Our Kindergarten Campus.*

Each day, five children would tell us some news about what they were doing or something about their family, and I would write it on a large paper, showing them the left-to-right and top-to-bottom method. I would "fly" the marker over the poster paper until they yelled for it to stop on the spot where I was to begin writing.

At the end of the week, we would rewrite their news stories on smaller paper and have the kids illustrate it and draw pictures of activities we'd done that week. They would draw the weather and pictures from stories we'd read. I'd copy it and send it home to the parents. It was a great way for parents to talk to their kids about what we had done and learned that week.

I learned very quickly that kindergarteners don't really understand filtering personal information. There were several times that I helped the kids think of something different to share because their parents might not have been too happy about some of the things they had shared with us.

One day, I called on Trenton to tell us his news. Each week, Trenton had a difficult time coming up with something interesting to say and would often say, "I dunno" or "I forgets." I would ask him several questions until we came up with something "newsworthy" to write about.

On this particular day, he had an answer. I had my marker all ready to write and said, "Okay, Trenton, I am ready for your news." Trenton was very excited and said, "Well, yesterday, I ranned into my mom and dad's bedroom to see if I could watch cartoons on TV, but they was *negged* and they yelled at me, 'Trenton, go back to bed!'"

I was writing as fast as I could, but stopped when I got to the word 'negged' because I wasn't sure what he was talking about. I asked him, "Trenton, what does *negged* mean?" He looked at me with his big, beautiful, blue eyes and said, "You know, *negged*. No clothes on — *negged*." Then he paused for a minute and thought about it, and then he yelled, "But only on Sundays!" I've discovered that when you spend all of your time around 6-year-olds, sometimes you get into a mode of thinking where adult information goes right over your head just like it does for the children.

Once I understood the translation of the word "*negged*," it took everything I had not to burst out laughing. He was so serious. He finally said, "That's some good news, teacher, huh?" Biting the inside of my cheek, I replied, "That is very interesting news, Trenton, but do you think your parents would be happy if we shared it with everyone and their parents?"

He thought about it for a minute and finally said, "Hey, my cat had four little kitties." I yelled, "Perfect!"

Every day, the news was fun to hear, but here are a few news bits that I felt I needed to help the kids edit as I thought they could be classified as TMI.

Paul: "My dad got kicked out of my brother's basketball game by the 'zebra man' because his mouth was too naughty, and he was yelling and yelling and yelling. My mom sent him to bed without any dinner."

Blythe: "My grandma and grandpa couldn't come to dinner last night because my grandma lost her teeth."

Jeremy: "I am not supposed to tell anybody this, but my mom ran into a car at Smith's and just drived away!"

Michael: "My little brother pooped in my mom's closet, and she hasn't even found it yet!"

Gene: "My dad and my uncle were wrestling around the living room last night, and they broke my mom's lamp. But we are not supposed to tell her. Ever!"

Sarah: "Sometimes my brother wears my sister's panties and dances all around the house." (The brother was 14, sister was 16)

Jesse: "My dad gotted so mad at the neighbor lady that he dumped our garbage right in her grass yard."

Jimmy: "My mom and dad got in a gigantic fight because my mom took the remote control to work and my dad missed his 'precious game.'"

Jack: "My brothers caught a huge snake, and they are hiding it in their room, but don't tell my mom because she will be a screaming crazy lady!"

7

BOBBY

Early on in my career, I began to realize that some kids are dealt a bad hand in life, and I thought it was a teacher's job to try to teach them that they were important and that they had the power to make positive choices for their lives. I thought that if I could teach them that, even though their life was a lemon, they had the power to make it lemonade. (I think I may have been the ever-optimistic Pollyanna in a previous life). Anyway, at least that is what I thought.

Until I met Bobby.

Bobby had three older brothers, all of them teenagers. Bobby was 5 years old, and he told me he had a different dad than his brothers and that his dad was even meaner than their dad. He told us that his 16-year-old brother was in "juvy" and that his other two brothers, who were 15-year-old twins, were headed there, too. He tried to act like he was a hardcore criminal like his brothers.

He told us that all his brothers had been in "trouble with the law" and that he thought that was really cool. He told me they all had "rap sheets." I had to call a lawyer friend to figure out what a "rap sheet" was, which ended up being a list of the charges that had been brought against them for crimes they had allegedly committed.

Bobby was a beautiful child. He had big brown eyes and black hair that he wore spiked up with his brother's gel. He had an angelic face and a beautiful smile. He wore a black leather jacket and torn jeans. He was super cute and looked like he had just walked out of the musical *Grease* or *West Side Story*. He could have been a T-Bird or a Jet.

At first, I was charmed by his little tough-guy act and thought he was adorable. He tried to talk tough, which came out as, "Hey, Teach. How's it hangin'? You lookin' fine today! You gonna teach me some BLEEP today or what?" He actually bleeped himself because his mother said he wasn't allowed to swear at school.

The other kids thought he was fun, too — at first! He would high-five them and taught them some "secret hand signs." (I later found out that they were real gang signs he had learned from his brothers.)

As the year progressed, the kids started coming to me to tell me that Bobby was pushing them and bullying them. I talked to Bobby about it, and he said that the kids liked it because it was making them tough.

I taught the kids about problem-solving and if Bobby did something inappropriate to them, they were to say, "Stop, Bobby! I have a problem with you [insert infraction here]. Let's talk about it."

This was a great skill to teach those kids because it empowered them to stand up for themselves and gives them words to fight with instead of having to use their fists. This usually worked well and cut down on the tattling and rough-housing and built bonds and friendships — usually!

Problem-solving became a cruel game for Bobby to punish the other kids with. He would count how many kids he could make try to "problem-solve" with him each day and how many kids he could push down or how many of their snacks he could smash or how many people's hair he could pull. His bad behavior was getting worse daily. He was a full-fledged bully. I tried to keep him away from the other kids. I would talk to him and try to figure out how to help him. The principal and I worked together to come up with a consequence we felt would change his behavior. We put him on a behavior plan that allowed him to earn good things for positive behavior. We tried positive reinforcement. We tried negative reinforcement. We tried everything we could think of. The harder we pushed, the more brazen he became and would brag about his misbehavior.

Eventually, he arrived at a point where he had no friends and no one would play with him. The other kids avoided him. The adults on recess duty had to watch him every minute. We were all very concerned and felt like we couldn't control him, much less reach him.

We tried to communicate with his mother, but when we could get her to call us back, she said that he was 5 years old and that 5-year-olds don't do the things we were saying he did and that it was our job to make him behave if he was. She blamed it on the other kids and said that they must have been bullying him for him to act like that. I knew she worked nights and tried to sleep during the day, but she refused to help us with Bobby. According to her, it was *our* job and *my* fault that he was acting out and it was me who had to deal with him. We tried to contact the father, but found out that he was in prison on a felony assault charge.

One spring day, while I was on recess duty, I noticed that Bobby was sitting on the railroad ties that surround our playground. He had a large piece of bark and was rubbing it on the railroad ties. I went over and sat by him and asked him how he was doing and what he was doing. I was trying again, for the hundredth time, to build a relationship with him — to let him know that I cared about him. He actually looked up at me, and I noticed he had tears in his eyes. He said sadly, "I don't got no friends, and nobody likes me, so I am going to kill them all!"

I was horrified, but tried to stay calm. I questioned him, "Tell me about not having any friends."

He said, "I hate everyone, and everyone hates me!"

I said, "You must have been bullied in your life because it seems like you know a lot about bullying. Is someone hurting you? I care about you and want to help. How can I help you, Bobby?"

All of the sudden, he stood up and started screaming at me. "Shut up, teacher! Just shut your mouth! I don't gotta talk about it. You're not my friend, so don't pretend that you are. I hate you, and I hate everyone at this school. No one here don't care about me at all." He stomped off and went behind the door and curled up into a ball and sobbed.

I knew this was out of my league, and I needed some help. The principal tried to help him and called the district psychologist for help, too. He really broke my heart. I had tried so hard to build a relationship with him so that I could teach him about empathy and to care about others, but he had built a solid wall around himself and was so unbelievably angry.

The next day, he showed up at school and acted like nothing had happened. He kept to himself, but did everything I asked him to do. He didn't interact with the other kids — or me, for that matter — but he didn't seem as destructive as he had been.

After recess, I sent the kids into the bathrooms to wash their hands. Most of them came back quickly, but there was no Bobby. Luckily, I was already on high alert and ran to the bathroom. As I got closer, I could hear him screaming, "Go ahead and cry, baby. You big baby. Boo-hoo, hoo! I am going to hurt you, and then I am going to hurt your whole family!"

As I burst into the boy's bathroom, I saw that Bobby had another little boy pushed up against the bathroom wall. He was holding the piece of bark that he had whittled into a rough-looking knife up against the other little boy's throat. The other little boy was shaking, and I wasn't sure he was even breathing. I grabbed Bobby's hand and made him drop the knife and gathered the other little boy up into my arms and started to rock him and make sure he wasn't cut. The little boy burst into tears and started to sob. Bobby just stood there like he was in shock or in a trance. He showed no emotion at all. He just stared at us. It seemed like time stopped. The only sounds in the room were Bobby's heavy breathing and the other little boy's desperate sobbing. I wanted to grab Bobby and shake him and then hug him and tell him that I cared about him and that he didn't have to be like his dad or his brothers, but his eyes seemed blank — like nobody was even in there.

Finally, he kicked the knife away and walked out of the bathroom and straight to the principal's office and slammed himself down on the chair. Carrying the other little boy who was still shaking, I followed him. The principal and the secretary were both there, kind of dumbfounded. Bobby finally said, "I think you better call the police. Now I will have a rap sheet, too!" He grabbed his knees and buried his face in them and then started to cry.

The police came. Bobby's mom came. They took him away to a different school for troubled children. He was the youngest person ever to attend that school. I've always wondered what awful things he learned there from the other troubled kids. I tried to keep in touch with Bobby. I wanted him to know that his kindergarten teacher cared about him and wanted him to be successful. His mom blamed me and insisted I not contact him ever again. I knew that I had failed him. I didn't have the skills to help him. I knew the other kids in my class paid a big price as I tried to help him. He took so much of my attention that I failed them. I spent many sleepless nights thinking through what I could have done differently — what I could have done better. He hurt my heart.

Years later, I ran into the district psychologist, and he told me that Bobby was in prison and that they had tried to get him some help for his mental issues, but that he had not responded well. I've wondered many times if some of the kids that have chosen to shoot up their schools began to show signs in kindergarten. I still feel a strong wave of sadness and failure when I think about that beautiful little boy I couldn't reach. I've wondered what he could have been if he had chosen a different path.

8

DAVID

The first seven years of my career were spent teaching kindergarten in the mornings and Title I math in the afternoons. My Title I classes consisted of six students at a time who came to me for 30 minutes. I would work with them to help them understand the math concepts they were missing. These kids were all from each of the upper grades, third through sixth.

My time was tight because I put the kindergarteners on the buses at 12:10, hoping all the parents were there to pick up their kids. Then I only had 30 minutes to clean up from kindergarten and prepare the things I needed for the math classes. I was also supposed to eat lunch. I had a class every half hour until the end of school. Needless to say, it was a tight schedule.

At 12:45, I had six fourth graders from three different classes who would come to me. I had visited with their classroom teachers and found out which specific skills they needed to work on. This was a lot of work, as I had to track each student individually and prepare a lesson for each one. I did this for all 24 students.

In my fourth-grade group, I had four boys and two girls. We did a variety of games and activities to help them grasp the needed skills. One of the boys was named David. He was darling. He had a mullet haircut that he liked to make look kind of scraggily. He had hazel eyes and beautiful, clear skin. He had a great smile and was the kind of kid that thought it was fun to cause a little trouble. He told me, "It gets ya noticed!"

He was a great kid and seemed to enjoy coming to class and really loved life. He was a little rambunctious and a little naughty in a playful-but-not-harmful way.

In fact, herein lies the problem. He was supposed to show up each day at 12:45, but he would sneak out of his classroom about five minutes early. He thought it was fun to hit all the papers hanging on the walls as he passed by and see if he could knock any down. He tried to get kids wet using the water fountain to spray them. He pulled all the stuff off the coat rack as he passed by. He just liked to goof around on his way to my class. When he arrived, he would sneak in and try to scare me, which he usually did. We'd laugh about it and then wait for the other kids to arrive.

Eventually, several teachers and staff members noticed his behavior and visited with me about trying to get him to stop. I talked to him about it, and he would laugh and ask, "What is the big deal? I'm not hurting anyone."

He wasn't trying to be destructive; he was just having fun. I asked him to stop, and he said he would try really, really, really hard. And then he winked at me.

He was a charmer.

Of course, his shenanigans continued. I received enough complaints that I had to talk to his classroom teacher about making sure he didn't leave the class until 12:44. He said he would try.

At first, it worked. He would show up to class on time and tell me he hadn't caused any problems all the way down the hall. We high-fived each other and then would go on with our lesson. He was a good kid and worked super hard on math.

One day, about a month later, he came into my classroom real early and scared me as I was eating lunch and getting ready for class. Unfortunately, I overreacted and forcefully said, "David, you're too early. Please go back to class until our class starts!" I knew instantly that I had hurt his feelings.

He stood in the doorway for a few seconds then finally snapped, "Okay, fine. But I am never coming back to your class again!" He stomped back down the hall.

Several minutes later, the other members of the class walked in. I asked the girl from his class if he was coming back. She said he returned to class very angry and told his teacher that he was never coming back. I felt bad about the confrontation but thought that I should let him calm down before I would visit with him and apologize the next day.

David died that night. The next day never came! I never got to apologize. David never came back! I was devastated. Our whole school was devastated, especially since the accident happened at school. He went to the afterschool program that day. He was playing basketball with one of the workers and accidently tripped and hit his head hard on the cement gym floor. They called his mom, and she came to pick him up immediately. She was a nurse and recognized that he had a hematoma, but the bump was not swelling out — it was swelling in and was affecting his brain. They were unable to relieve that pressure in his brain fast enough.

My daughter was in his class and was his friend. Their teacher handled the death with kindness, compassion, and understanding, but it took months for the kids to begin to heal. It meant a lot to my daughter that their teacher let the kids know how much he was hurting, too. They had many class discussions and sharing times about how much they missed David. It was a tough year.

I went to David's funeral. I was so impressed with his parents. You could tell that they were hurting, but were very careful to not blame anyone and made sure that everyone knew it was an accident. His mother hugged me and thanked me for being his "funnest" teacher. She told me that he would show her the games we played in class and the "super cool" skills I taught him. They were so gracious and kind after such a tragedy. I was amazed. They were really good people.

Our student body planted a tree in David's memory. The tree is still growing, and when my daughter visits the school, it brings backs the sad memories, but it also reminds her of the good times she had with her friend David.

I learned how important it is to never, ever let a child leave your class after you have said something you know you will regret. Solve it then and there, or you may never, ever get another chance. Regret is a terribly heavy burden.

9

KALANIE

Kalanie had turned 5 years old the day before the deadline for kindergarten registration. She and her parents had just moved to Pocatello from Hawaii so that her father could finish his master's degree at our local university. She was very young and very, very tiny.

Her father explained to me that he and his wife were both born and raised in Hawaii and were very excited to move to a place where they could experience all four seasons. They had told Kalanie about the leaves changing colors and new plant and flower growth in the spring, but mostly, they were all excited to see snow. None of them had ever seen it and couldn't wait until the first snowfall happened. They asked me how soon it would actually snow in Idaho. I assured them it wouldn't be long and told them they might even have a white Christmas. They were so excited.

Our school is located on a hill on the west bench of our city. It has a great view of the whole entire city. It's a great place to have a grade school except on days when it's really windy and any day it snows. There are two roads leading to the school, both very steep and dangerous for buses and cars to try to maneuver up, especially on icy, snowy days.

The school district is very hesitant to call "snow days" because it's inconvenient for parents, so there have been many, many days that teachers, buses, and parents struggled to make it up that hill to get their children to school.

In my 23 years of teaching, I think we only had about eight snow days. I asked the superintendent once what it takes to have a snow day. She said there are three things that a storm must have in order to call a snow day: wind, ice and, lots and lots of snow. If they don't have all three for several hours, then we have school.

Our staff used to laugh at school districts that would cancel school because they got an inch of snow. We were covering up extreme jealousy. In my opinion, there were many days that should have been snow days because it was very dangerous to bring the kids up our hill because of the weather. We had tons of accidents and scary fender-benders. Also, because we were on a hill, it was often very, very windy.

The first time Kalanie got to see snow was on a particularly cold day. It had snowed several feet the night before and was piled everywhere. They hadn't called a snow day because the wind had stopped blowing, but it was still a yucky mess. Our janitor literally had to dig pathways for the kids to be able to get into the building. In some places, the snow had been piled higher than my shoulders.

Kalanie was thrilled. She was so excited because her parents had bought her brand-new snow clothes. She was adorable in her new coat and snow pants and her pink Hello Kitty hat, gloves, boots, coat, scarf, and earmuffs. It took us a good five minutes to get her dressed for recess. When she walked outside, she reminded me of the little boy in the movie *A Christmas Story* because she could barely walk with all the clothes bundled on her.

It had been very cold, and the wind was picking up, but we decided to go out and play for a few minutes anyway. In Idaho, recess is very important to all children. We deliver recess like the post office delivers mail: neither snow nor rain nor dark of night could keep us from our recess plight! (Except we've never actually had recess in the dark of night, but you know what I mean.)

I held onto Kalanie for the duration of recess so she didn't tip over or blow away. Only her dark brown eyes were showing, and I could hear her giggle under the scarf that was covering her mouth. It was windy, but she sure loved the snow.

Upon our return to class, I helped her peel off her layers of winter clothing, and I asked her what she thought of the snow. She giggled and said, "Teachew, I am weally confewsed. How do you get it to snow sideways in Idaho? I thought snow was supposed to fall down because of gwavity." I laughed hard and hugged her and explained that usually it does fall down, but because it was so windy, it was blowing sideways. She said, "That is weally sad because I heard I could make a snow wangel."

The storm got worse and worse as the day went on. At noon, we bundled up all of the kids and walked them out to the buses. I walked out with the other kids while my aide helped Kalanie get all her winter gear on. It was so windy and snowy that the kids had a hard time walking to the buses, and several of them fell or slid across the ice. I was very relieved when they were all safely on the bus, and I prayed that someone would be there to meet them when they got off the buses.

About 20 minutes after the buses had left, I was called to the office for a phone call. It was Kalanie's mother, and she was very, very upset. I was having a hard time understanding what she was trying to tell me. It took several minutes for me to be able to figure out that she was saying that Kalanie was not on the bus when she went to pick her up. I immediately panicked and put out the "all-points bulletin" to search the school to find Kalanie.

All the para-pros, the principal, the secretary, the janitor, and all available help went searching for the pink bundle of tiny little girl. We checked every classroom, bathroom, lunchroom, closet, library, nook, and cranny in the school. We called the bus driver, but he didn't remember seeing her. We could not find her. To say there was a school-wide panic would be an understatement. It's my worst fear as a teacher to lose a child. It was a horrible feeling for everyone.

Kalanie's mother had called her husband and then called the school back and was on hold while we searched the school. I was in tears as we all decided that we needed to call the police. As the secretary called the police on one phone, I went into the principal's office to tell Kalanie's mother we were calling the police.

As I was standing there, fretting and trying to talk to her, I looked out the window and saw the most beautiful sight I had ever seen. Kalanie was hugging the flagpole. The snow was piled up on three sides so we could not see her from outside. The side closest to the building didn't have snow piled in front of it, so I could see her. She was hanging onto that flagpole for dear life. The wind was blowing her so hard that she thought she was going to blow away, so she clung to the pole with all her little strength.

I yelled into the phone, "I see her! She is stuck to the flag pole!" and hung up the phone. That was not one of my proudest professional moments, and it really confused Kalanie's mom because she immediately called back to find out what had happened.

I ran to peel Kalanie off of her life pole. I hugged and hugged her and carried her back into the building. Her hat was frozen to her hair, and her eyelashes were frozen. She was like a little pink popsicle. I grabbed a blanket and some warm water, and we warmed her up the best we could. I sat and held her and rocked her until her parents got there. When they arrived, I handed her to them, and they hugged and hugged her.

Her dad asked her, "Kalanie, are you okay?"

She explained that she was trying to walk to the bus but the wind "blowed" her right away, and she had to hold onto the flagpole until her teacher found her, but her teacher took a long, long time, but she knew her teacher would come and help her very, very soon.

She thanked me for saving her, and then she said, "Snow and wind in Idaho is weally, weally scarwy!"

It was a rough introduction to snow, but as the year went by, Kalanie learned to love it. The kids showed her how to build a snow fort and how to make snow angels. She even took pictures and sent them to her friends in Hawaii, who were amazed. The thing I can't figure out is how that tiny little girl even got to the flagpole; it was completely surrounded by snow. She told me the "snow wind blewed her there."

10

VENICE

One fun activity we did in kindergarten was a homework project I would have the parents complete with their child. They would find a baby picture of their child and tell them why they chose their name.

The kids would get up and tell us the story behind their name and show us their baby picture. Most of the parents wrote the explanation down so that I could help their child remember if they forgot. It gave the kids an awesome chance to speak in front of the whole class and to work with their parents on fun homework.

It was very interesting to find out how many children were named after relatives or friends or movie or sports stars or musical groups. There were also a lot of Bible names.

One thing that I always thought was interesting was that five years after a new Disney movie came out I would have a child with the new character's name in my class.

I have taught several Ariels, Belles, Jasmines, Tianas, and even a Nahla. I look forward to a few years from now when I will have an Anna and an Elsa. Thank you, *Frozen*!

One year, I had a little red-headed girl named Venice. She had big blue eyes and adorable little freckles all over her nose. She was darling and spoke very well and was fun to listen to because she articulated her words carefully.

I called on her to tell us about her name and show us her baby picture. She went to her backpack, but could only find the picture. She explained that her mom had written a paper with the information about her name on it, but she couldn't find it, so she would try to remember what she had told her.

She said, "My mom is a travel agent and helps people plan awesome trips to places all over the world. Sometimes, she earns enough points that she and my dad get to go on special vacations. She said that every time they go on a trip, my mom "convinces" a baby so they name the baby after the place they went."

I repeated what she said, questioning what she meant. I asked, "She *convinces* a baby? What does that mean?"

She said, "I'm not sure, but that is what she said!"

I thought about it for a minute, then asked, "Do you have any brothers of sisters?"

She said, "Yes, I have an older brother named Boston and a little brother named Houston. Oh, and my mom is having a baby sister named Cheyenne at Christmastime."

A light bulb finally went on in my head. The word she was looking for was *conceived*. I didn't explain that to her, but I thought it was very funny.

As she sat down, she said, "Oh yeah, teacher, my dad said to tell you that they aren't ever, never, ever going on any more vacations. Period. And he means it! NEVER!"

11

JENNIFER

One of my biggest concerns as a teacher is that one of my students gets injured at school. It's a daily concern because teachers are so outnumbered, and it's difficult to keep your eye on 25 students at the same time and still teach. Believe me — it's a lot of responsibility to protect *all* your students *all* the time.

Inside days are the trickiest of all. If the weather is below 10 degrees or if it's pouring rain outside, or if there has been a ton of snow, but not enough for a snow day, or if the playground is covered with ice or if there is a moose on the playground, especially a baby moose or a mama moose looking for her baby (yup, it has happened three times at my school), or a mama deer with her babies wandering through, we keep the kids inside. To say the kids get a little stir crazy would not accurately illustrate the scene.

Our school lets the teachers decide what the kids are allowed to do on inside days. Some teachers have the kids sit in the hall and read books. Other teachers have their kids go into the library to watch a movie and go to the lunchroom and visit after they eat breakfast. A few teachers even let their kids into their classrooms to play floor games or catch up on work.

When I first started teaching, I couldn't decide what I wanted to let the kids do, so I kind of let them decide. Big mistake! My kids were all over the building, and some of them were not making good choices. I should have known something bad would happen.

One day, we had a windy, yucky, messy, cold day. It should have been a snow day because the parents and buses couldn't get up the hill to school. There was a lot of excitement in the air because there had been many fender benders and small accidents and everyone had a story to tell about how hard it was getting to school that day.

Most of my kindergarteners were in the lunchroom eating breakfast and jabbering away. Some of the older kids started running around the lunchroom. We were short several teachers and para-pros (the aides who watch the kids before school starts) because they were stuck behind buses that couldn't get up the hill. It was mayhem!

The janitor, bless his heart, was trying to clean up the lunchroom, which was a horrible job because the kids were wild and running around. He was trying to put up the tables and benches and lock them into place on the wall. We had retractable tables that fold in halfway then are lifted up into a space on the wall, where a latch holds them in place.

He was also trying to mop the floor so that our P.E. coach could start his first class as soon as the bell rang. The coach usually tried to help the janitor get the lunchroom ready, which was nice and not in his job description, but that day, he was not able to get up the hill either.

I was in my room trying to comfort children who had had harrowing experiences getting to school that morning. The kids were all talking at once. One little boy was explaining that his dad's truck had slid into their mailbox, and a little girl said that her mom's car slid back down the hill and ran into the stop sign. One little boy told us that some policemen had to push his grandma's car up the hill. It was a mess.

Right before the bell rang, one of my boys ran into the classroom yelling as loud as he could, "Teacher, Teacher, come and help! The table broke Jennifer's face! Teacher, Teacher, hurry! You have to help Jennifer! The table broke her face!"

I followed him into the lunchroom, and there sat my little, beautiful Jennifer holding her face with blood squirting out through her fingers. The kids told me that one of the sixth graders was running and had slid into the table the janitor had just put up and the latch had released and the table slammed down just as Jennifer was walking by and hit her right in the face, knocking her to the ground.

It was a horrible sight. I grabbed Jennifer up in my arms and immediately started reassuring her that she was going to be okay. I was trying to figure out where her injuries were to see if I needed to apply pressure. She wasn't even crying because she was in shock. I asked one of the kids to go get the principal and another one to go find some ice. Of course, all the kids went screaming to the principal's office.

By now, Jennifer and I were both covered with blood. One of the kids had grabbed a clean towel from the lunch ladies, and I held it on her face while the lunch ladies were getting some ice. The principal asked me if we needed an ambulance. I said, "I think we do!"

She went to call 911 but soon realized that the roads were blocked by cars and a bus trying to get to the school.

Jennifer's little face was a mess. She had a cut over one eye, her nose was bleeding, and both eyes were almost swollen shut. She was a wreck, and I was really worried about the accident affecting her neck and even her brain. She wasn't crying. She was just moaning and holding onto my hand as I held the towel on her face. It was a really scary feeling. I kept talking to her as calmly as I could and telling her she was going to be okay and that we were calling her parents and they would help us. I was panicked inside but didn't want her to know that. We were both shaking.

The decision was made that the police, who were helping with the traffic problems, would drive her to the hospital and meet her parents there. I really wanted to go with her and thought I should, but it was decided that the other kids in my class needed me, as they were all traumatized, too. It was truly a tough decision. I stayed at school, but to this day, I'm still not sure that was the right decision because when I handed Jennifer off to our school counselor and the police to accompany her to the hospital, she started to bawl. It was horrible as I realized one of my greatest fears had come true, and I knew I couldn't help her anymore. I wish I had gone with her.

At the hospital, they x-rayed her face and discovered that the table had broken her eye socket and crushed the cartilage in her nose. She had gotten whiplash in her neck. The doctors were very concerned that she had gotten a concussion and were watching her very closely for that.

When Jennifer came back to school, she looked like she had been on the losing end of a very bad boxing match. Her nose was bandaged, she had two nasty black eyes, and her face was badly bruised. She also had a few stitches in her forehead. I was a little hesitant to see how the kids would treat her when they saw her and felt very protective.

We talked about what had happened so that the kids knew it was an accident and that Jennifer hadn't done anything wrong. I said, "Unfortunately, she was in the wrong place at the wrong time."

One little boy named Jake said, "You mean, she was in the wrong place with the wrong table at the wrong time?"

At first, the kids just stared at her. I took her hand and lifted her onto my lap so that she felt protected. Bobby, one of the toughest, cutest, coolest kids in my class, stared at her and finally said, "Jennifer, you are the coolest-looking girl I've ever seen. I really like your face, and I don't even like girls."

Thank goodness Jennifer laughed, and then all the kids laughed. They all started asking her questions at the same time. They thought it was cool that she got to go to the hospital in a police car and that she got to go to the hospital. They all had a story to tell her about their experiences with hospitals and the police. She was a real trouper. She listened to everyone and answered everyone's questions and ended up feeling really special.

At first, Jennifer's parents wanted to sue the school district, but they all came to a settlement to cover all the costs for treatment and any future plastic surgery. The best thing that came out of the whole experience was, now, not only do the tables and benches latch in place, they also lock them. I made sure that the kids knew Jennifer was the hero and that she helped make the school a safer place for everyone.

About six weeks after the accident, I heard Bobby go up to Jennifer and smile and say in his tough little, cool voice, "Hey Jennifer, by the way, I like how your face turned out!" She blushed and ran to me to tell me what he had said.

It was super cute, and I gave Bobby an extra big thumbs up. He reciprocated with a thumbs up back to me. He really was a cool kid, and she was an angel. There was some lasting trauma, and Jennifer's parents wisely got her some counseling.

By the way, now, on inside days, my kids are allowed in my classroom so I can protect them a little better!

12

ALICIA ANN & ALAN

Alicia Ann was the whiniest child I have ever taught. She had a real nasally, high-pitched voice, and she used it to whine about everything. She whined about being too tired and having to get up in the morning because kindergarten was too early. She whined because her pencil wasn't sharp enough. She whined if she wasn't first in line. She whined because she was hungry. She whined if I didn't read the book she wanted, or if she had to do hard work, or if the sun was too hot, or if it was raining or snowing or blowing. It didn't matter what it was — she would find something to whine about. It felt and sounded like fingernails on a chalkboard whenever she spoke.

Every day, the other kids would beg me to get her to stop whining. Many times, I would call her over and quietly ask her to try not to whine because it was hard to listen to and annoyed the other kids. She yelled at me as loud as she could and whined, "I! Am! Not! Whining! My dad Says I whine, too. BUT I DO NOT WHINE!" She would stomp away and pout.

Alicia Ann was a beautiful child. She had blonde hair that reached past her waist when it wasn't pulled up. She had crystal-clear blue eyes, high cheekbones, and a strikingly beautiful face. She was always dressed like she had just stepped out of a fashion magazine. To look at her, you would think she was a model. She was tall with graceful long legs and arms and a remarkable smile. I was struck by how breathtaking she was until she spoke — I mean — until she whined. It seriously felt like someone was poking needles in my ears.

The kids in the class would ask me to help them problem solve with her to try to get her to stop whining. Her answer was always the same: "I do not whine!"

It was frustrating for everyone because we would try to help her, but she was convinced that she didn't have a problem, but that we did!

Alan was a chubby little Hispanic boy. He described himself to me once as "jolly." He would say, "I have a lot of jolly in me!" He was delightful and clever and loved to learn and have fun. He had big brown eyes and jet-black hair. The other children were drawn to him because he was so much fun. He loved to giggle, and his laugh was infectious. He loved life and was joyful until he had to deal with Alicia Ann. She annoyed the heck out of him, and she knew it.

It was an interesting thing to watch. He was usually a really happy-go-lucky kid, but as soon as Alicia Ann was anywhere in his vicinity, he would become annoyed. He would kindly say, "Please take your whining somewhere else" or "I do not appreciate your whining today." Of course, she would shout, "I do not whine!" He even tried to demonstrate how to change her voice to not be whiny. She covered his mouth with her hand and told him to stop because she didn't whine.

One day, Alicia Ann came to school, and she had darling pigtails sticking straight out of both sides of her head. They fell past her shoulders like golden waterfalls. She was dressed in a blue-and-white-striped overall skirt with a blue shirt underneath. She had blue bows tied around her pigtails. She was adorable. She was even wearing blue-and-white socks and shoes to match. She skipped into our classroom, pigtails bouncing with every step.

All day long, she flipped her pigtails around. She thought it was awesome that she could whip people in the face with them if she stood close enough. I asked her several times to stop hitting people with them. She squealed and then whined that it was fun. Soon the kids just stayed away from her as much as possible.

Towards the end of the day, we were cutting out snowflakes to hang from the ceiling. It was a great activity that I used to teach congruence and line of symmetry. The kids were working away and doing a great job. I was hanging them as they finished when I noticed that Alicia Ann and Alan were sitting next to each other at a table. I heard Alan say, "Stop, Alicia Ann! I have a problem with you flipping me in the face with your hair. Let's talk about it!" She would giggle and then do it again. I heard him ask her several times.

Finally, I walked over and kneeled by Alicia Ann and said, "Please stop flipping Alan with your hair. He has asked you several times to stop. It's annoying him and frustrating the other kids at the table. I will have to move you if you don't stop." (I should have moved her.)

She started whining and said she was not doing it on purpose. No one believed her. I said, "Please stop accidently flipping him in the face with your cute pigtails, please!" She nodded!

When I turned around to hang up some more snowflakes, I heard the loudest, most annoying and high-pitched scream I have ever heard. I spun around and saw a shocking sight. Alan was sitting at the table with a shocked look on his face and one of Alicia Ann's pigtails in one hand and a sharp pair of scissors in the other. Alicia Ann was standing next to him screaming as loudly as she could. She sounded like someone was murdering her. I was stunned! Everyone froze and stared at Alan. My mouth fell open as I tried to form words.

Alan's eyes filled with tears, and he whispered, "I asked her ten times to stop, and I just couldn't take it anymore!" He dropped her hair and the scissors and put his face in his hands and wept.

Alicia Ann kept on screaming. My para-pro ran to Alicia Ann to try to calm her down, and I tried to comfort Alan. It was a mess. We walked them both to the principal's office. My para-pro then returned to the classroom to take care of the other kids.

The principal looked at me in disbelief. I was holding Alicia Ann's pigtail and the scissors, Alan was sobbing, and Alicia Ann was still screaming. The principal calmly asked Alicia Ann to stop screaming. She wouldn't, so the secretary took her into another room, shut the door, and let her continue screaming. We called both sets of parents and asked them to come to the school. I don't think I have ever dreaded meeting with parents as much as I did that day.

Alan's mother arrived first, and he melted into her arms and continued to weep. Both of Alicia Ann's parents showed up about five minutes later. Her dad stooped down, looked her in the face, and pointed his finger at her and briskly said, "Stop screaming right now."

She stopped instantly. I was amazed. Her father put his hand kindly on her shoulder and patted her lovingly.

He whispered in her ear, "It's going to be okay. We will work it out."

We all gathered in the principal's office. The principal explained that we had had a problem in kindergarten today and turned to Alan and asked him to tell everyone what had happened. He tried to take a deep breath and finally whimpered, "I couldn't take it anymore. She whines and whines at me all the time, and today, she kept flipping me in the face with her hair."

He turned to her parents, and with tears rolling down his cheeks, he said, "I even asked her ten times to stop!" He buried his face back into his mother's lap and wept.

Alicia Ann started to scream again. We all covered our ears. Her father took her by the arms, turned her to face him, looked her in the eyes, and said, "Stop, right now!" She did. He then said directly to her, "Alicia Ann, your mom and I love you so much, but I have explained to you several times that everyone hates your whining. It's annoying and frustrating to people. I knew that someday your whining would cost you big. I have no idea why you would continue flipping him in the face with your hair when he asked you to stop, but this behavior has got to end. Your mom and I want you to have friends, but you can't treat people the way you have been. No more. I mean it. No more whining, no more annoying people, no more. I mean it this time!"

Her dad turned to the principal and stuck out his hand to shake it. He then shook my hand. He nodded to Alan's mom and rubbed his hand on Alan's head. He turned and picked Alicia Ann up, thanked us for our time, and said, "We will take care of this."

He walked out of the office and out of the building, with Alicia Ann's mom following him, saying, "But, but, but..." And then they were gone.

We all watched them go and stood there in stunned silence except for the sound of Alan's weeping. The principal sat down in his chair and handed Alan a tissue and said, "Alan, what do you think we should do about this?" With his little tear-stained face and broken voice, he stuttered, "I really didn't mean to cut her hair. She was just so annoying. I asked her to stop. I tried to problem-solve ... I mean ... I mean ... the devil made me do it!"

I couldn't help it, but I burst out laughing. His answer surprised me so much that I laughed out loud and had to walk out of the room. That devil is a tricky little bugger.

It was decided that Alan would have to stay in for the next several recesses and write Alicia Ann an apology letter. He was truly repentant and wrote the cutest little letter. In the letter, he did ask her to stop whining and told her how cute she looked with her new shorter haircut and that he wanted to be her friend and that she was fun when she wasn't screaming or whining.

I wish I could say the whining stopped, but it didn't. However, we did convince her that she did whine and that she needed to start policing herself. Alan tried hard to be her friend but would walk away whenever she started whining, which helped her realize how much she did it. By the end of the school year, she had cut her whining in half and was working on stopping altogether with a lot of help from Alan.

PART II

TEACHING SECOND GRADE

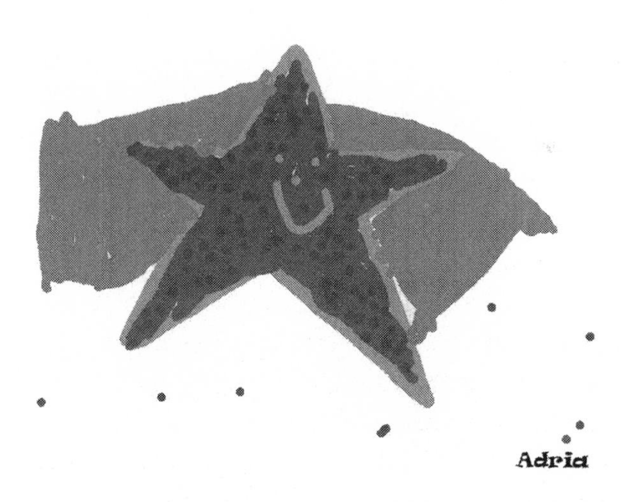

13

CHRISTEN

One of the big risks of being a school teacher is the continued opportunity we have of sharing germs with sick kids. I have had kids wipe their noses on me, sneeze in my face, throw-up on my neck, and get diarrhea all over my shoes. Unfortunately, a lot of parents don't have childcare options, so even if their child is sick, they send them to school anyway.

Having said that, I hate missing school, so if I did end up toughing it out and teaching through the sickness, I tried hard not to spread germs. It's just too much work to prepare for a substitute. But every once in a while, even if I do wash my hands continually, I lose the germ battle and have to stay home.

There was one day when a little girl named Kayla was rubbing her eyes. They were really red and swollen and looked infected. I said, "Hey, sweetie. Come here and let's wash your hands and try not to touch your eyes anymore, okay?"

I was getting some hand sanitizer ready for her when she walked over and put both of her little hands on my face, saying, "Teacher, thanks for always being so nice to me and taking care of me. I telled my mom my eyes hurted, but she said I haved to go to school anyway."

After school, I called her mom and asked her to please take her to the doctor, as I thought her eyes were infected. She did, and they were. And now so were mine. I had tried to wash my face and hands, but the infection had spread to one of my eyes.

I went to the doctor, and he confirmed that I had an infection in my left eye and that I was contagious, which meant that I needed to miss at least the next two days of school. Then, he dropped the big news. He told me I could not wear makeup until the infection was completely cleared up and that I had to throw away all of my makeup and buy new stuff.

Yikes. That was super bad for me. I am a strawberry blonde with very, very pale skin. I have white eyelashes and eyebrows and freckles everywhere on my face. In fact, I pretty much have no face when I am not wearing makeup.

It ended up taking two days to be able to return to school. On the third day, as I was meeting the children at the door and telling them how glad I was to be back and to see them, I noticed that some of them were staring at me.

Christen, a delightful little rolly-polly boy (his words, not mine) could not take his eyes off my face. I tussled his dark hair and smiled at him and said, "Well, good morning, Christen. I am so glad to see you today." He just stared and waved.

We went on with our morning activities, but I noticed that Christen just kept on staring at me. After several minutes, he came over to me. He pulled on the sleeve of my shirt. I looked at him, smiled, and said, "Howdy, Christen. How can I help you?"

He stared at me and finally said, "Wow, teacher. I had no idea how important makeup is to your face!" He was not trying to be mean. He was just completely perplexed and dumbfounded.

I laughed hard and hugged him, but I think that kind of scared him a little. He just went back to his desk shaking his head.

A few days later, I was finally able to wear make-up again. When Christen saw me he said, "Now, that is the face we all know and love!" We both laughed.

14

BRYCE

One morning, as I was bringing the kids in from recess, I noticed adorable little mop-topped Bryce was sobbing. I went to him and said, "Bryce, buddy, it looks like you had a rough recess. Would you like to report about it, or were you able to solve the problem yourself?"

Through his tears, he said, "I tried really hard, Teacher, but I'm not even sure what happened."

"That's a tough one. We'd better talk about it," I responded.

It's my personal opinion that it's really important to teach kids to solve their own problems, if it's at all possible. I truly believe it's empowering to children. Problem-solving is an amazingly powerful tool. It's a great way to get kids to identify their feelings and feel powerful without bullying. At the beginning of the year, we practiced a lot, and it's worked well and helped the kids build great relationships. I used little finger puppets to teach them the words to say to solve a problem before they were allowed to tattle.

Over the years, I have had many parents ask me about problem-solving and how they could get their other kids to do it as well. I also tell the kids that listening to tattling makes my ears bleed. They think that is pretty funny.

To me, tattling is different than reporting. I have found that most injuries in second grade are accidents. Kids accidently run into each other or trip and fall. Some kids crowd and push each other but, I teach them to stand up for themselves. When I sat down with Bryce, he lay his head on my shoulder and tearfully said, "Dustin and I were playing with a ball, and we both tried to grab it at the same time. Then he pushed me down and called me a *Mormon,* and I don't even know what that means."

By now, a lot of my kids were gathered around because they were concerned about Bryce. Crying was out of character for him.

A little girl named Sabrina rubbed his back and lovingly said, "Bryce, it's okay. It's good to be a Mormon. I am a Mormon, and it means that Heavenly Father and Jesus love me and want me to choose the right and be happy. I am really happy to be a Mormon."

A couple of the other kids agreed with her and told us they were Mormons, too, and it was a good thing. He felt a lot better about it.

He did tell me that he had tried to solve the problem with Dustin, but that he wouldn't listen to him. He just pushed him down and called him a Mormon and ran away.

After I walked the kids to lunch, I asked Dustin to come and talk to me for a minute. The conversation went like this:

Teacher: "Hey, Buddy. I heard you had a little problem with Bryce at recess. Can you tell me about that?"

Dustin: "He stole my ball, and we were fighting, and then he accidently fell down, and then he was yelling at me."

Teacher: "Did that make you feel bad?"

Dustin: "Yes, he is my friend."

Teacher "Did it make you feel better to call him names?"

Dustin: "I shouldn't have done that, though. He just made me so mad!"

Teacher: "It does sound like you were pretty frustrated. That was an interesting name you called him. Tell me about that."

Dustin: "My brother calls me that all of the time."

Teacher: "How does it make you feel when he calls you a Mormon?"

Dustin: "It makes me really mad because he is so mean about it."

Teacher: "What do you think a Mormon is?"

Dustin: "I have no idea. He is just really mean and it makes me feel bad."

Teacher: "So, you wanted Bryce to feel bad like you do when your brother calls you that?"

He nodded.

Teacher: "I'd like you to think about it tonight. Think about how bad you feel when your brother does it and see if that is really how you want to make your friends feel, okay?"

We shook on it.

The next day, Dustin came in kind of excited and said to me, "Teacher, I want to talk to Bryce and solve our problem from yesterday. I talked to my brother about it, and I want to fix it."

When Bryce walked into the room, Dustin ran to him and said, "Stop, Bryce. I felt bad when we were fighting over the ball yesterday, and I shouldn't have pushed you, and I especially shouldn't have called you a Mormon. My brother calls me a moron. I was supposed to call you a moron not a Mormon because that is being mean, but I didn't mean either of them, so I'm really sorry, and I want to be friends again."

Bryce was thrilled that they were friends again.

The funniest thing happened after that. Sabrina walked up to them and said, "Now, you two sound like Mormons. We all try to be nice and friends with our neighbors." Then she skipped away. It was so fun to watch them work it out.

15

JUSTIN

Every year, I get so excited to meet the new students with whom I get to spend 170 days. Each child is like a little puzzle to me. I love to figure out how they learn and process information. I love to learn about their family dynamics and how they interact with me and the other kids. It's seriously one of my favorite parts of my job. I just love putting each little person-puzzle together in my mind.

Occasionally, I have had the opportunity to have a child in my class who was completely different from any other child I have taught. Every child has awesome qualities and delightful talents and personalities, but sometimes, I get a child that just knocks my socks off.

One year, I had a little fireball named Justin. He had dark hair and huge brown eyes. He had a remarkable sense of humor and an amazing sense of timing. Every day, he would say funny things that he wouldn't even mean to. He just had a remarkable way of looking at the world.

It took me a while to teach him not to blurt out what he was thinking because it disturbed the other kids, so we came up with a plan. When he thought of something clever to say, he would raise his finger and wait until I saw it. Occasionally, his finger did a little crazy dance because I didn't notice right off, but once I did, I knew he would say something that would be a treat for the whole class.

During the first two or three days of school, I was having four or five kids come to my table so I could work with them on reading in a small group while the other kids were reading to themselves or with a partner in a whole group setting. I didn't know all the kids' names very well yet, so this is the conversation I had with Justin and the other kids:

Teacher: "Thanks for coming to work with me, kids. I am going to see if I can remember all your names. If I don't, you get a sticker! I believe your name is Sarah, and you're Amy, and you're Kory and you are ... Justin."

Justin: "Let me check." (He turned around and looked.) "Yes, ma'am. That is indeed the name on my underwear."

Teacher: (laughing) "Your name is on your underwear?"

Justin: "Yes, ma'am. It's how I tell my underwear apart from my sister's underwear."

Teacher: "You can't tell your sister's underwear apart from your underwear. Really?"

Justin: (snickering) "Teacher, are you accusing me of wearing my sister's underwear, because I never do ... anymore."

Teacher: "No, I am just surprised you can't tell them apart."

Justin: "I can, you silly! Hers say Jessica!"

We all laughed and laughed. Finally, Kory said, "Justin, it's easy to tell the difference between girls' underwear and boys' underwear!"

Justin: (exasperated) "I know because our names are on them. I check every single day!"

We all knew he was pulling our legs, but he was just so clever and delightful about it. This was an everyday experience. He just came up with funny stuff, and his timing was impeccable. He was never mean; he was just so clever.

One day, he said to me, "You know, Teacher, when I grow up, I want to be just like you ... except I'm going to shave or maybe have a mustache, and I'll have short hair and some hair on my chest and not wear dresses and stuff. And absolutely no makeup. Okay, okay. What I meant to say was, when I grow up, I'm going to be nothing like you except that I'm going to be nice and kind just the way you are! That is actually what I meant to say."

This little boy made me smile every single day. His first-grade teacher told me he had a horrible home life. He and his twin sister, Jessica, were living with their father, who had just gotten out of prison, and their mom had just been arrested and was going to prison. They had been in foster care and had been handed around to different family members for the past two years. He had very little stability in his life.

At the end of the year, I said to him, "You know, Justin, you are going to do great in this world because you have such an amazing outlook on life and such a super attitude."

He responded, "Thanks, Teacher. But I am going to do great in this life because my second-grade teacher taught me my ABCs and 123s. What else could any kid possibly ask for?"

16

COLE

Good, caring, supportive parents are a gift to a hard-working teacher. It's always such a joy to meet parents who say, "How can I help you educate my child?" I love having parent volunteers help in my classroom. I always have them run a learning station and they always tell me how much they appreciate what I do and they had no idea how challenging and enjoyable teaching is.

Kids who have parents who care about education and talk to them about school, specifically what they are learning, usually have respectful, engaged, bright students.

Unfortunately, some parents don't even know their child's teacher's name or what grade they're in. But there are some parents who know which specific skill they are working on in math and which book the teacher is reading to them and what level their child is in reading. It's always amazing to me to think of the number of children I've taught and the number of parents I have never met. I spend six hours a day with their child, and they don't even take the time to come to school and meet me. They don't come to parent-teacher conferences or class meetings or school activities. In my opinion, there is a direct correlation between how involved a parent is and how their child does in school. Thank goodness, most parents are interested in their child's learning and support their teachers.

One of my favorite families I've ever taught had six children. I taught the five youngest because I wasn't teaching yet when the oldest child was in my grade. They had three boys and three girls. When each of their children entered my class, they already loved reading. I could tell their parents read to them every night. They told me that they had math time each night also. Each child shared what they were working on in math at school. The parents practiced handwriting and spelling with their kids. They taught their kids that they were lucky to be able to go to school and that they were extra lucky to have teachers who cared about their learning.

By the time each of their children came to second grade, they had a favorite author and a favorite genre of books. Their parents required them to give book reports to the whole family and write an opinion about the book and try to talk the other kids into reading their book.

The mother often contacted me to find out what we were working on in language arts, and then they would work on it at home. Their kids were excellent students and loved school because their parents taught them how important education was.

They served on parent-teacher committees and supported all the school events. The mother was often in charge of the school book fairs, which helped raise money to buy books for the library. They were the kind of family that all schools love to have in their boundaries. Their kids knew that education mattered to them. Both parents had graduated from college and let their kids know they were headed there as well.

Cole, the family's youngest child, was a delightful, quiet young man. He had big, dark eyes and straight dark hair. He was a thinker. He worked very quietly and pondered all new information. He loved to learn new things and would often discuss new learning with me. He especially loved science and wanted to learn everything about the earth and loved learning about space.

Cole would share with me his opinion about each book he read and would explain to me why some kids in the class might not appreciate a given book because they might not have as much "background knowledge" (his words) as they needed to understand the given subject. He wasn't annoying, and he didn't think he was smarter than anyone else — he just said he "thinks a lot about stuff because he has been read to so much, and the other kids like to play more." (Their family didn't have a television and didn't play video games.) He was actually very interesting to talk to. He loved to be challenged, so I would try to find books he hadn't read before and offer them to him. They were usually a little bit above his reading range, but his siblings and parents would help him decipher words and meanings until he understood. He said it helped his brain grow.

One day after spring break, Cole came into class a little early in the morning before school started. He said, "Good morning, Teacher. I am glad to see you and very glad that school has started again."

I replied, "Cole, I am thrilled to see you and am very excited that you're back and ready to learn more interesting stuff."

Thoughtfully, he answered, "Teacher, I spent most of spring break thinking a lot, and after much deep thought I have decided ... that school is a pretty good use of my time!"

I laughed out loud. He was kind of befuddled by my reaction, so I quickly said, "Cole, that makes me so happy because it's wonderful to have a student that has decided that school is worth his time. Well done, son!"

He nodded, turned around, and went out to play. He warmed my heart.

17

BRENDA

Show-and-Tell has always been one of the highlights of my classroom. I have a few rules for Show-and-Tell: 1) No toys or electronics; 2) The object or talent must teach the other children something; 3) The child must be able to identify the educational discipline the item fits into (math, science, reading, social studies, history, music, P.E., etc.); 4) Each child has an assigned day, and they can only show on that day. If they don't have something ready, then they have to wait for the next week to share.

Many parents thank me for having Show-and-Tell because they work with their child all week to come up with something to share. I have had kids bring pets, baby clothes, antiques, fossils, bugs, rocks, family pictures, money from other countries, maps, flags, and the list goes on and on. I have had kids write songs and play the piano or guitar. Kids have shown us karate kicks and dance moves. It has been a lot of fun and great learning.

One of my favorite Show-and-Tells ever was from a little girl named Brenda. Her father had been stationed in Afghanistan all year. She worried about him every day. We visited a lot about how amazing he was for fighting for our country and how hard it was for him to leave his family and friends. It was a really scary time for her, so I let her talk to us about it whenever she needed to share. Her favorite thing to say was, "Hey class, my dad isn't dead today!" Her mom had some way to communicate with her dad so that he could let them know that he was alive and well. Those days were filled with joy for Brenda. There were days, however, when he was on a mission and couldn't contact them, and she would spend the day worrying about him.

We had several class discussions letting all the kids know that Brenda's dad was fighting for our country and was helping keep America safe and free. The kids thanked her every time, which did help her feel better, but she still always worried about him.

In March, when her dad came home, she asked me if he could come for Show-and-Tell. I said, "Absolutely! As soon as he can!" She was so proud to introduce him and explain to the kids that he had been fighting for our country and that he was in danger a lot. He wore his fatigues and brought his helmet and gear. (He knew he was not allowed to bring his guns into the school.) He showed the kids on a map how far away he had been from home. He explained what he did and that he was in the special ops division of the Army, and while he was in Afghanistan, he had to carry a rifle to protect himself and others and that the rifle was almost as tall as they were. The kids were entranced.

One of the most fascinating things he explained was about the people in Afghanistan. He said the people were afraid of the soldiers at first, but when they figured out that the Americans were trying to help them, he said they were very kind. He brought a burka and scarves and explained that the women always kept their faces covered to show respect for their husbands. He showed the kids what it would look like by putting all the clothing on Brenda. We could only see her eyes. The kids thought it was so cool, and we could hear Brenda giggling behind her veils. She was adorable.

The last part of her Show-and-Tell was an Army Humvee. Her dad had arranged with the Army to be able to bring it to school to show the kids. We all went outside, and he told them all about it. He even let them sit in it. He explained that the taxes their parents pay help pay for the amazing things the Army has, and that is how we help people all over the world. He told the kids that America has the best, strongest Army, Navy, Air Force, Coast Guard, and Marines in the whole world and that we should be very proud of that because we help tons of people.

It melted my heart to watch Brenda listen to her dad. She stood up tall and had a huge smile on her face the whole time. She was so incredibly proud of him. It was awesome to watch.

After he had told the kids all the fascinating information, I asked the kids if they had any questions for Brenda or her father. One little boy raised his hand and asked, "So, Brenda, what is your favorite part about having your dad back?"

She responded, "That is easy. Now when I pray at night, I thank Heavenly Father for bringing him home safe instead of asking Him to make sure my dad didn't get 'blowed' up in Afghanistan!"

To which her dad responded, "When I pray at night, I am thankful that He helped me get home to Brenda, and I am extra glad I didn't get 'blowed' up in Afghanistan either!"

The kids were very interested in Brenda's Show-and-Tell and asked her tons of questions about it for weeks. She told them how scared she was when he was gone and how happy she is now that he is home and how proud she is that he is a veteran. It was so heart-warming to watch her talk about it because we had listened to her worry and fret about him for all those months that he was gone. She told me that she was so excited to tell her dad that three boys in our class told her that they wanted to be soldiers just like her dad was when they grow up, and one boy was still thinking about it, but he probably would, too.

18

HEIDI

Heidi was a beautiful, golden-haired child with crystal blue eyes. She usually wore a long braid down her back. She was quiet and very bright. Her parents helped her pick out unusual items to bring to school for Show-and-Tell.

One time, she brought in some money from Brazil that her father had gotten when he served a mission there for The Church of Jesus Christ of Latter-day Saints. She brought a map and showed us where Brazil was, and she explained that their government was very different from ours. She also showed us a Brazilian flag and a soccer shirt. She explained to us that soccer is really, really important to the people of Brazil. We were all really fascinated.

Heidi had the cutest lisp. The speech pathologist was working with her, and she was overcoming it, but it was still adorable when she talked.

One day, she had a Show-and-Tell I will never forget, not because it was so unusual, but because of the way one of the other kids reacted to it. It was a very interesting exchange.

Teacher: "Heidi, did you bring a Show-and-Tell to share with us today?"

Heidi: "Yeth, Teacher, I did. Thith ith a picture of me and my dad on the day I got baptithed."

Johnny: "Oh, what did your dad do to have to go to jail?"

Heidi: (shocked) "My dad didn't go to jail. Anywayth, it wath really thpecial to me becauth we wore all white, and my dad baptithed me by immerthion, which meanth he dunked me all the way under the water, and that wathed away all of my thinth, and I am very clean.

Johnny: "Oh, did your dad hold you under the water? Is that why your dad had to go to prison because that is really bad?"

Heidi: (frustrated) "My dad didn't go to prithon." (She looked at me to help her, but I shrugged my shoulders because I wasn't sure what Johnny was talking about either.) "It wath a really thpecial and beautiful day becauth my whole family wath there, and I got a new dreth. In my church, we get to get baptithed when we are eight yearth old and know we can chooth the right."

Johnny: "Well, I don't know how your dad got a white jumpsuit in prison because my dad's is orange. All he ever gets to wear is an orange jumpsuit. Maybe that's the color you wear when you do drugs."

Heidi and I just stared at each other, and all the kids stared at Johnny. It was such an interesting exchange because Heidi could not picture anyone in prison in any kind of jumpsuit, and Johnny could not imagine why anyone would wear a jumpsuit (white or any color) outside of prison.

This exchange was such an interesting view into the dynamic of my class and how differently they looked at life. I always try to teach the kids about empathy and acceptance and about not judging others.

After Show-and-Tell that day, Heidi and Johnny had a very interesting conversation that I could overhear.

Johnny: "I liked your Show-and-Tell. Your dad looks really nice."

Heidi: "He is the best dad ever. Sorry your dad had to go to jail."

Johnny: "Yeah, I know, but he is not really that good of a guy. You're lucky to have such a good one."

Heidi: "I'll bet you could come over sometime, and my dad would be nice to you and maybe even play ball with you like he does with my brother and me."

Johnny: "That would be cool. I wish my dad was like that. You're so lucky. I'll bet good dads are awesome!"

19

DUSTIN

Every child I have ever taught has made an impression on my life. I spend nearly nine months out of the year, six hours a day, five days a week with each child. I work hard to build a relationship with them. Occasionally, it's a challenging quest, but usually, it's a delight to get to know each little person. I love to figure out how they think and how they feel and especially how they process information. It's truly the most enjoyable part of teaching. I have taught a few children that I am convinced will change the world.

The first time I saw Dustin, he was limping down the hall of the school. He had long golden hair past his shoulders. He was tall and very thin. When he walked, he would drag his left foot. He still had breakfast food on his face, and his shirt had Spaghetti O's and macaroni and cheese on it. His pants were cream colored, and it looked like he had spilled punch or something red on them. He was a mess, but he had a huge smile on his face.

He said to me, "You're my new teacher, and I am so happy to finally meet you. I hear great things about you and know we are going to have a great year."

He shuffled past me and then turned around and said, "Oh, my name is Dustin, and it's a beautiful day to start school."

That was Dustin. If you could ever describe a person as a little ray of pure sunshine, that was Dustin. He was always happy and smiling and had the most positive attitude I have ever seen in a child. The thing that amazed me the most about him was that he really had a terrible life — at least by my standards.

He lived in a two-bedroom duplex with his two older brothers and one little sister and his dad and his grandma. It was his grandma's place, which he told me he was grateful for because he didn't really like living at Aid for Friends (a homeless shelter), but that the people there were super nice and gave him food and sometimes even played games with him, and he really appreciated all they did for his family. But he liked living with his grandma because she loved him even though she yelled at him a lot and never cleaned the house because she couldn't walk.

He told me his mom had "drug issues," but that she was going to get help when she got out of jail. He told me that she was really a good person, but that she got in with "a bad crowd," and they talked her into doing drugs. He said that sometimes his dad takes him to see her on visiting days and that she always kisses him right on top of his head and says, "You be a good boy, my little Dustin, because you are extra special, and I love you!" He would tell me that he couldn't wait until she got off drugs and got out of jail in October and could stay with her.

He asked me once if I knew why his mom thought he was extra special. I said, "Because you are a little ray of sunshine in a dark, dark world!"

He giggled and said, "No, it's because I drag my foot when I walk, and I can't run like the other kids. Did you know when I was a baby I had a clubbed foot? The doctors tried to fix it and accidently cut my Achilles tendon, and so my foot drags. But that made me different and super special because none of the other kids are like me."

I replied, "That is true. You are special, but it's because you have such a happy spirit and such an amazing brain. I love the Lamborghinis you design." He smiled and said, "You are a cool teacher!"

Because Dustin couldn't run or play very well, he spent recesses visiting with me and telling me about his family and especially about his dreams. He told me that after he graduated from high school he was going to college and he was going to get a degree in mechanical design, and then he was going to work for the Lamborghini company and design awesome, amazing cars. He would show me the pictures he drew of these amazing cars he had designed. He told me he dreamed about them when he slept and then in the morning he would draw them. I was truly amazed at his talent. He told me that sometimes when God takes away something from you like the use of your foot he makes another part of you stronger like your imagination. He amazed me every day.

Tragedy struck his family at the end of October. Dustin's dad showed up at school and checked all the kids out. We found out that their mom, who had recently been released from jail, was found dead from a drug overdose. It was shocking and devastating to all the kids. The school counselor and I knew the situation the family was in financially and decided to buy the kids some clean, nice clothes to wear to the funeral. We bought the little sister a beautiful dress and the boys all nice shirts and pants and new shoes and underwear. We delivered the gifts to their house but were horrified when the oldest brother opened the door and we could see how filthy it was inside. We stepped inside the door but could go no further because it looked a lot like hoarders lived there. There was no place to go. Dad came out, and we explained what we had brought. He graciously thanked us and shut the door. It was super uncomfortable.

Our counselor and I went to the grave-side service and watched this little family grieve. They looked so great in their new clothes, but they were so sad. We wished we had bought them coats because it was a cold, drizzly day. Grandma sat on one end of the seats, and Dad sat on the other end, and the kids were lined up between them.

It was a really touching sight. It was easy to tell how much Dad and Grandma loved those kids.

As soon as Dustin saw us, he limped over to us as fast as he could and gave us huge hugs and smiled and thanked us for the awesome clothes and told us that he loved, loved, loved his new shoes. He usually had to wear special shoes because of his foot, but these fit him. He told us that he was sad about his mom, but that she was in a better place and was probably a lot happier.

Then he said, "Teacher, who is watching the other kids? I know they're being good, but I am worried. What if they need your help? I don't want you to get in trouble." I reassured him that I had gotten a substitute so I could come to the funeral. That was Dustin — worried about me and all the kids in our class.

We visited about his mom during many recesses. He told me that he didn't think she was ever happy in her whole life and that she should have decided to be happy because she had great kids.

He asked me, "Teacher, how come some people just don't decide to be happy?"

I had to tell him that I honestly didn't know but that I wished more people would choose happiness like he did.

In December, right before Christmas, another tragedy struck. Dad showed up at school again and checked all the kids out of school. He had gotten home after working the midnight shift and found Grandma dead in her bed. This devastated the family again, as now there was no one to help Dad with the kids. The school counselor and I went to that grave-side funeral again. This time, we had bought the kids new coats.

Once again, Dustin came over to thank us, and once again he was worried about the kids and that he really appreciated that we came to help him. And once again, he told us that his grandma was probably a lot happier in Heaven. I told him that I knew his heart hurt and that he would miss his grandma a lot. He told me that he was glad he had some good memories with her and that his memories would get him through. Oh, my goodness, this kid was 7 years old. I could not believe all he had been through in his life.

Shortly after his grandma's death, during one of our recess discussions, I asked him if it was hard to be happy all the time when bad things kept happening. He looked up at me and thoughtfully said, "You know, Teacher, I've thought about that a lot because some really bad things have happened in my life, but then I think some really great things have happened in my life, too, and I choose to remember the great things instead of the bad things. It's a choice. I'm weird like that." I smiled and thought I wish we were all weird like that.

In January, Dad came to me very sad and explained that he and the kids had to move out of our school boundaries because he was not allowed to stay in his mother's house without her. My eyes began to tear up as I looked upon this broken, distressed man. He worked so hard to help his kids and had to deal with tragedy after tragedy. He told me how much he appreciated what I had done for Dustin and how much his little boy loved me. He thanked me for being "the only continuously positive woman in Dustin's life" and explained that when he gets home from school he always talks his head off about how I smiled at him and listened to him and that I believed in him and that I knew he would work for Lamborghini someday. It seemed to me that I had done so little for him and that it was just part of my job, but it made a huge impression on me about how much the little things I say and do matter.

Dad came to visit with me on a Wednesday. Dustin didn't come to school for the rest of the week, so I knew they had had to move. I was broken hearted and worried so much about him all weekend. My little Dustin was gone. My little ray of sunshine was shining in some other classroom. What was going to happen to him? Who was going to look at his sketches and ask him about his cars? Who was going to remind him to wash his face? Who was going to giggle with him about all of the different food groups he had on his shirt? I knew it was completely selfish on my part because I knew, with his attitude, he would be fine anywhere he went, but I was so very sad and missed him terribly.

It was truly one of the happiest days of my career when, on

Monday, he and his dad came into my classroom and explained to me that their counselor had encouraged them to do whatever it took to keep him in my class because they all felt it was so important to have a "consistently, positive female" in his life with all the tragedy he had been through that year. The school district had decided to leave him with me. I was thrilled. He had come so far in his academics, too, and I knew he was such a positive influence on all the kids in my class. They embraced him as he came back into the fold.

Dustin told me one time how important the kids in our classroom were to him. One recess, he explained to me that, a few months before, some sixth graders were bullying him before school. He said, "You know, Teacher, that has happened a lot to me in my life. Some kids were calling me "gimpy" and making fun of me and walking like me. But did you know that the kids in our class surrounded them and told them that they had a problem with big kids picking on their friend and they needed to move on?"

He continued, "I really think we have the best class of all of the second-grade classes ever made. I am so glad the big kids didn't pound on them."

I chuckled, "Me, too!"

We had a discussion after that with the whole class. I told them how impressed I was that they helped Dustin.

Sean said, "You taught us to, and besides, he is our friend, and nobody gets to pick on him, and I mean nobody."

He laughed. I asked them how it felt in their hearts when they helped him.

Kerry said, "It was a little scary, but I loved it. They were big kids, too, but I am never going to let people tease other people. It felt good to help."

Little Mr. Sunshine spoke up and said, "You people make me proud to be people. Thank you for being my friends."

Dustin finished the year with us. During our recesses together, he would tell me that some days he really missed his mom and his grandma and his house (they were living in a trailer park now), but that every day he was so grateful for his dad and his brothers and his sister and his teacher and his friends and his neighbors and his dog. Then he said, "And the list goes on and on."

On the last day of school, as I gave Dustin a huge hug, I asked him, "Who is going to be my little ray of sunshine from now on, Dustin?"

He smiled and said to me, "You can remember me forever, and Teacher, always know that happiness is a thing you choose."

20

LEIGH

It's really hard for me to admit, but there are some kids that are a puzzle to me. I usually go to great effort to try to figure out how each child learns and processes the world around them. I try to understand their family's dynamics and how it affects their learning. But try as I might, there are a few kids I just cannot understand.

Her name was Leigh. I knew she'd had a tough life. I knew her mother had lost custody of her when she was a baby and social services had given her to her ailing grandmother. I knew that her mother had shown up again when Leigh was in kindergarten with a 2-year-old brother and tried to take control.

Leigh explained to me that if her mother could get custody back of her then she would get the money the government paid her grandma to take care of her. Leigh's mother did get the government assistance for her brother, but the grandma got it for Leigh. Leigh didn't understand the process and thought she should get the money and spend it how she wanted to. Leigh thought her grandma was ripping her off and her mom was trying to steal the money that Leigh thought should have been hers.

Leigh would brag about how she abused her grandma. Leigh said she would hit her grandma and run away because her grandma couldn't catch her. Leigh loved to pull Grandma's hair and laugh at her. Leigh loved to make her grandma mad. I just could not understand how and why Leigh could be so cruel and then brag about it. The other kids tried to explain to Leigh how horrible her behavior was towards her grandma, but she just laughed. Her behavior was so weird.

Leigh didn't have any friends because she was so nasty. She was a very thin, tall girl. She had long, stringy brown hair. Leigh told the class that she broke the brush because her grandma tried to comb her hair. I know her grandma tried to help her, but she often looked very unkempt. Leigh was often dirty and would wear the same clothes day after day. She refused to let her grandma help her clean up and change her clothes.

Leigh was in charge at her house no matter what her grandma said. When I visited with Grandma, she would show me the bruises Leigh had inflicted on her. We tried to get Grandma some help, but the option the social services had was to give Leigh back to her mom. But Leigh's mom abused Grandma, too.

On Halloween, both Mom and Grandma showed up for the school costume parade. While the other kids were lining up, Leigh's mom and grandma got into a huge fight in the hall. They were screaming obscenities at each other. I have never heard such foul language in my life, especially in front of kids.

The thing that struck me was the look on Leigh's face. Leigh was sitting in the hall watching them fight. Grandma had pulled Leigh out of class to put makeup and her costume on her, but apparently, Leigh's mom wanted to do that, too. Leigh seemed to really be enjoying the fight. She had that Cheshire cat smile on her face and even snickered a few times while her mom and grandma were screaming at each other. It was disturbing.

Mom and Grandma both tried to grab Leigh. They started pushing each other, and Mom finally pushed Grandma down. One of the other kid's dads helped her up. He was shocked. I finally had to try to break them up, which was ridiculous because I was trying to prepare my kids for the parade. I had called the principal, and he got there as soon as he could and asked them both to leave. Leigh's mom turned on him and called him some pretty nasty names and refused to leave. We ended up having to get the police involved.

It was ugly.

A few days later, I asked Leigh about the confrontation. She said, "It was awesome. My mom is a great fighter, and my Grandma is such a wimp!"

I explained that her grandma was trying to help her and really cared about her. She said, "My grandma is crap! She is stealing my money!"

I couldn't believe it. I kept thinking, *I want to go to the Wonderful Wizard of Oz and get this girl a heart.*

Leigh was a very good reader. Her grandma had taught her. A second grader is supposed to be able to read 92 words per minute fluently by the end of the year, but she was reading 110 words per minute right on day one.

I told her how impressed I was with her reading.

Leigh said, "Whatever. Reading is dumb."

The thing that was so odd about Leigh was that she read 110 words at the end of the year, too. She had no growth in reading throughout the whole school year. I talked to her about it and asked her what she thought of that.

She said, "I don't really care. Reading is for losers."

I tried to not be accusatory about it, but was very stumped by her reaction. Leigh could have been so amazing and could have learned so much more. She didn't comprehend most of the things she read. She read for speed only.

Leigh refused to help any of the other kids with reading or math or anything. In fact, as the year went on, we had to keep her away from the other kids because she would hurt them physically or say mean, horrible things to them, or steal and then ruin other kids' things. I tried so hard to understand this little girl's thinking process and how she processed relationships. We talked a lot. She was very open with me about things, but the way Leigh explained her feelings was not normal for a second grader.

Here is a perfect example: One of the boys in my class had just received a brand-new coat for his birthday from his grandparents. It was a very expensive brand, and he was thrilled to show it to the other kids. He even got gloves and a hat to match. At recess, he was talking to the other kids about it. The teacher on duty explained to me that she noticed Leigh watching him. We had all been trained to keep our eyes on Leigh because we never knew what to expect.

It was a windy, slick day, and one of the kids had fallen on the ice. The recess teacher was helping the little boy. Leigh noticed she wasn't watching and ran towards the little boy and grabbed the back of his coat and swung him around until she ripped his coat off. Once Leigh had it in her hands, she took off running. The teacher noticed and started blowing her whistle to get Leigh to stop. The teacher said Leigh turned and looked at her and saw the teacher coming and threw the coat up in the air as hard as she could. The wind caught the coat and carried it into the neighbor's backyard, where the neighbor's dog tore it to shreds. Leigh laughed and laughed. She thought it was hilarious. The recess teacher told me that everyone just stood there and stared at her, horrified at her reaction. Leigh refused to apologize. Her grandma felt terrible about the whole thing, but knew she could not afford to replace the coat. The PTO is an organization that includes parents and teachers working together for the good of the school. They paid half of the money, and I paid the rest to replace the coat.

Leigh was not allowed to go out to recess anymore with the rest of the students. She hurt too many people and did too much damage. She ended up spending recess and lunch in a fifth-grade classroom, which she loved.

One day, I asked Leigh to come and have lunch with me. She was happy to because I think she knew that I cared about her and she would talk to me. She wouldn't talk to the other adults or would just respond with "I really don't care" to any adult who tried to ask her questions about her behavior.

We visited about her life. Leigh knew I didn't approve of how she treated her grandma, and I let her know that I refused to listen to her brag about it, so she didn't discuss it with me. We talked about her little brother and her "crazy mom" and how she actually liked school, which stumped me. I asked her to explain.

She said, "I like your class because we do fun, interesting things. I like the songs we sing and the stories you read us, and I love the math." Leigh almost sounded like a normal kid.

As soon as I felt like we had a good, trusting conversation going, I asked her, "Leigh, will you please explain to me about how you think about things? You seem to really like it when I tell you that you're doing well in reading, math, writing, and all the other subjects. You're such a smart girl and could do so many great things in life."

She nodded.

Then I said, "Can you please explain to me why you do things that are so mean to the other kids? I am really trying to understand why a little girl that has so much potential chooses to do so many destructive things."

Her answer truly, truly shocked me.

She looked me right in the eye and said completely honestly, "Teacher, you don't understand. I really don't care if it's for good behavior or bad behavior. I just really like attention — everyone's attention!"

I said to her, "Leigh, I really appreciate that you're honest with me. I would so much rather give you positive attention than negative. I hate it when you get in trouble. I get so disappointed in the choices you make. You're so smart; you could be such a great kid if you wanted to be." She just kept on eating, completely unaffected.

She finally looked at me and said, "I know!"

That was it. She just stopped talking. Finally, after about 10 more minutes, the bell rang. The conversation was over, and that was the last time we really had a heart-to-heart talk.

Several years later, I learned that Leigh's mother had gone to jail for drug possession. Leigh and her little brother had both gone to live with Grandma, but they were abusing their grandma and hurting her so badly that they had both been removed and were in foster care.

Over the years, I have wondered if it's possible for a child to be a sociopath at such a young age. I have taught very few children in my career that truly could not understand how other people feel and were unable to learn or understand empathy.

There is part of me that hopes with all of my heart that Leigh — somehow, someday — will remember that her second-grade teacher believed that she could change her life for good because she was so smart. In fact, I still believe that.

21

JAKE

Jake had brown eyes and curly brown hair. He was quite athletic for a second grader. He was built like a football player: strong shoulders, thin waist. He had adorable freckles all over his nose. His birthday was in the fall, so he was one of the older kids in my class. He was one of those kids you liked to have around. He was always busy and friendly and loved to learn. He especially enjoyed recess. He loved being active.

One Tuesday morning, one of the other teachers who had recess duty brought Jake in to me and said, "Ms. Melanie, we have a problem. Jake got hurt on the playground. Can I please turn him over to you?"

I said, "Of course, I'd love to take care of my little Jake!" I was thinking he had a little booboo and needed a band aid. I wish that had been the case!

Jake had his face covered with both of his hands, and blood was seeping through his fingers. I said, "Oh my goodness, buddy, what happened?" I was horrified as he lifted his head from his hands. They were full of blood, and lying right in the middle of the pool of blood was his large, permanent front tooth. I was shocked, but I tried not to panic.

Several years earlier, I had visited with a good friend of my parents, who was a dentist and a terrific guy. We were at a party, and we sat, visiting about my decision to become a teacher. For some strange reason, he asked me, "So Melanie, do you know what to do if you ever have a student who knocks out a tooth?"

I responded, "Good question, what should I do?"

At the time, I thought that was a strange question to ask someone, but I was so very grateful that he had. That knowledge came back to me as I was trying to help Jake. I remember saying, "Wowzers, Jake, it looks like we might need to get a little help." I was trying to calm him down. I told him to try to take some deep breaths and not to put his tongue in the hole where his tooth had been. I remember what my dentist friend had told me so long ago and followed his advice.

Jake was hyperventilating. I had him look me in the eyes and talked calmly to him. I said, "Everything is going to be alright. My dentist friend told me what to do." We walked down the hall, trying not to get blood on the carpet. My stomach was in knots, and my heart was beating a mile a minute, and I was rubbing Jake's back, saying, "Everything is going to be okay — I promise. Everything is going to be okay." I knew he was going into shock, so I was trying like crazy to keep him calm.

The secretary called his mom and informed her about the accident and encouraged her to call the dentist. I kept reminding Jake not to let his tongue go in the hole. I had him spit into the sink, and I remembered that the dentist had told me not to put anything into his mouth. He had said, "Don't let him rinse out his mouth. Don't put any water in it. Just have him spit out the blood. You can put a cold paper towel on his lips, but don't put anything at all into his mouth. Try to keep him calm so he doesn't throw up." I had to remember to keep breathing as I was reminding Jake to keep breathing.

One of the para-pros had run to the lunchroom to get some milk. She said that we were supposed to put the tooth in milk because it's made of calcium like the tooth is and that it would help preserve the tooth.

Jake was a trouper. He didn't cry and just kept looking at me as I helped him remember to breathe. I kept putting cold compresses on his lips and reminding him not to let his tongue go in the hole. He really did a great job while we waited for his mom to show up.

Jake's mom walked in the door and informed us that she had called the dentist and that she was supposed to take him there immediately. Jake started to cry. He was very scared. I knelt down and said, "Jake, remember, everything is going to be okay. They will help you get your beautiful smile back." He calmed down and nodded and then quickly walked to the car with his mom's help.

Once Jake was seat-belted in the car and on his way to the dentist, I started to shake and hyperventilate myself. It was then when I remembered that I had 24 other kids I needed to worry about. Luckily, my awesome team of teachers had realized what was going on and had divided my students up and reassembled them in their classrooms. I love how we always had each other's backs and would step in to cover each other's classes if there were an emergency.

When I talked to the duty teacher, she told me that Jake had been playing tetherball and that he had slipped on the gravel and fallen face first into the tetherball pole. He had taken the full impact on his mouth, but she hadn't realized it had knocked out his tooth. She thought it had just cut his lip. She felt horrible about the whole thing. We all did. Her first instinct was to have him wash out his mouth, but decided to turn him over to me instead.

Later that afternoon, Jake's mom brought him back to school to show us what the dentist had done to him. She told us that we had done everything right. The dentist had told her that, because of our actions, he was able to save the tooth. Not putting anything into his mouth kept germs out. He was especially impressed with the fact that we had not let him contaminate the hole with his tongue, which allowed him to replant the tooth. He also said that putting cold compresses on his lips helped keep the swelling down.

She told us that once the swelling went down that the dentist was going to put braces on his teeth to keep them from moving, but that it would be able to reattach easily. She thanked us and let us know that it helped a lot that we were able to keep him calm and not let him go into shock. The dentist was amazed that he could help Jake without anesthetizing him. She told us that Jake kept saying, "Miss Melanie said everything was going to be okay and that I needed to breathe, and so I breathed, and everything is okay!"

I was so relieved. Later, I called my dentist friend and thanked him over and over again for that long-ago discussion and information. He was impressed that I had remembered it. He did tell me that the only thing that I could have done better was to have actually put the tooth back into the hole in his mouth instead of into the cup of milk, but that I could remember to do that next time.

There better never be a next time!

22

KAYLA

Another year, a little girl named Kayla quickly became synonymous for all things drama. She was a pretty, little second grader. She had an adorable face with shoulder-length straight brown hair and big brown eyes. But, holy cow, could she ever bring on the drama.

If something didn't go her way, she would plant her feet on the floor and start to wail. One time, someone accidently hung their coat on her hook. She turned around and let out the biggest, loudest 'Waaaaaaaaaaaaaaaaaaaaaaa!' I'd ever heard. It took me several minutes to even figure out what she was upset about. It was very disruptive to the whole class.

This wailing happened at least two or three times a day. I would take her aside and ask her to please stop wailing. I explained that if she would use her words, we could help her solve her problems faster and easier. She agreed, but then the next day, it would start all over again. It seemed like it was something she couldn't quite control.

I noticed quickly that there were no tears with these episodes. It seemed like it was purely an attention-seeking behavior, so I explained to her that I was going to start ignoring her until she started using her words. I told her that the rest of the class was going to do so also. I informed her that her behavior was hurting our learning and asked if that is really what she wanted to do. All of the sudden, she let out a huge "Waaaaaaaaaaaaaa!" right in my face. I was totally taken aback. Completely frustrated, I forced myself to walk away.

The other kids in the class became unbelievably frustrated with her and the constant wailing. They would come to me and ask me to make her stop. They asked why she couldn't solve her issues and make herself stop wailing. I asked them for suggestions on how to help her stop. One of my little boys named Jerry blurted out, "Duct tape. My dad says duct tape can solve any problem." Everyone laughed, even Kayla, but several students supported his idea. They even asked Kayla if that would work. Her reaction?

"Waaaaaaaaaaaaa!"

One day after Kayla had broken her pencil and started to wail, a little boy named Josh stared at her then put the back of his hand on his forehead, tipped his head back and, with a high-pitched voice, yelled, "Ohhhhh, drama!"

Everyone, including me, stopped and looked at Kayla. She stopped and stared at Josh. He smiled and did it again.

"Ohhhhhh, drama!" he said.

Shocked, Kayla started to laugh. Then everyone started to laugh. I asked Josh where he learned that, and he said, "Carol Burnett. She is a funny lady on TV, and sometimes, she says, 'Oh, drama!' and puts her hand on her forehead, and it reminded me of Kayla." It was brilliant and fit the situation so well. Thank you, Carol Burnett.

From then on, whenever Kayla had one of her moments, the whole class would lay their hand on their forehead and altogether say, "Ohhhhhhh, drama!" Kayla would stop and then do it herself. It turned out to be a really fun thing and helped a lot.

As the year went on, I began to notice that Kayla became more and more withdrawn. She would be very quiet and keep to herself, but then, four or five times a day, she would have these wailing bursts. It was almost like someone flipped on a switch, and the "Waaaaa" would just burst out of her.

I invited her to be my lunch buddy. She was thrilled and came in and sat down and started to eat. She noticed she had forgotten her napkin and started to wail. I calmly said, "That is not going to work for me. You're going to have to use your words, or you're going to have to go to the lunchroom to eat." She stopped immediately. I asked her, "Kayla, you can be such a delightful young lady. Can you please explain why you do such an annoying thing?"

She very calmly and straightforwardly said, "Because I have a secret, and sometimes it fills up my head, and I don't want it to come out, so I have to scream to keep it in, or it will blow out of my mouth."

I was dumbfounded.

She went on very matter-of-factly, "It's a bad secret and sometimes I think my head is going to explode!" She went on eating as if she was talking about the weather.

This piece of information explained so much to me about her behavior and the odd bursts of frustration. I said, "Kayla, I am so glad you told me that because now I know that you're frustrated about something and not mad. I understand that you have a secret, but if you ever feel that you need to tell someone or talk about it, I am here for you and will help you if I can."

She said, "Okay," and then went on eating.

We talked about her family. She told me that she and her mom and her three sisters had just moved from Wyoming and that her dad was still there building them a house. She said they moved to Pocatello to live with her aunt and her husband and their two babies. They all lived in a two-bedroom house, and it was really squishy. She said that she and her mom and all her sisters had to live downstairs and that there was only one bathroom and it was upstairs and that her mom and her aunt fought all of the time, but that her uncle tried to be nice and "keep the peace."

She said, "It's tough to have three grown-ups and six little kids in one tiny house." I agreed with her that it must be tough and that it was nice of her aunt and uncle to let them live there.

She said, "I know. I wish my mom wouldn't yell at my aunt all of the time. She is a nice lady." She went on. "My mom and my dad fighted a lot, and I hate it when my dad hits my mom. Although, sometimes, I just want to hit her myself." Then she slapped her hands over her mouth and ran out of the room, leaving her half-eaten lunch behind.

I think her secret may have just accidently fallen out of her mouth.

I cleaned up Kayla's lunch. For some reason, I expected a positive change in her behavior when she returned. Well, to say the least, I was very wrong. When the kids came back into the classroom after recess, Kayla's drama became much worse. Her wailing sessions doubled. When the kids would jokingly, dramatically sigh, "Ohhhhhh, drama," she would scream at them to stop. This really confused them because, before, she had laughed with them. We were all very stumped.

Our school counselor visited with her several times. Kayla would tell her that she had a secret, but that she couldn't tell it. When I visited with her, I explained that I think I already knew her secret. She said, "No, you don't. Nobody can know!" I told her she had accidently yelled it at me and that I understood that sometimes she feels like she wants to hit her mom, which is understandable to feel, but that she could never do. Kayla knew her dad shouldn't hit her mom either. I told her that I understood how confused she must feel about wanting to protect her mom and at the same time not wanting to get her dad in trouble. I said that that was a lot of grown-up problems to put on a little kid. She just stared at me for several seconds, and then she started to laugh.

She shook her head, rolled her eyes, and then ran outside to go to recess. I was perplexed.

As Christmas approached, we started talking about traditions and what our families did for Christmas. Kayla sat very quietly and listened, which surprised me a lot. She refused to answer the question when I asked, "Please, Kayla, tell us about your family's Christmas traditions." She turned and walked away. She paced around the room for a while. I decided to let her go because I could tell she was deep in thought and trying to work something out. The other kids continued to share. I noticed that Kayla crawled under a table and pulled her knees to her chest and started to rock back and forth. I watched her closely, but I didn't interrupt her.

When our sharing time was finished, we all went back to our desks to write about our discussion. Kayla remained under the table.

A little while later, I noticed that she had fallen sound asleep. She was such a beautiful child, but carried so much hurt. I was struggling to help her. There were times that I thought she was going to blow like a volcano, but instead, she would let out the wailing "Waaaaaaaaa," which seemed to calm her down a bit.

I could tell she was very distracted. When I talked to her about what we were learning, I could tell she was listening and interested, but when it came to doing seat work, which is work they do by themselves, or concentrating on something, she seemed to tune out. Her mind would immediately go somewhere else.

I noticed that she began spending more and more time under the table in the fetal position, which really alarmed me. Our counselor came into our classroom when she was doing this and talked to her about going into her office to visit with her. The counselor told me that they talked a lot about her family and that she was really worried because she didn't know what Christmas would bring. She really wanted to see her dad, but she couldn't because of the secret.

Christmas got closer and closer, and Kayla's behavior got stranger and stranger. We were making gifts for our parents, but she didn't want to make anything. When I asked her about it, she just shrugged her shoulders and climbed under the table. I knew that abused children often are told to keep secrets, so I was trying to build a relationship with her so that I could get her some help. She would not open up at all.

On the last day of school before the Christmas break, we were painting wrapping paper to wrap the gifts that the children would be giving to their parents. Kayla wanted to paint, so I got her the paper. She wrote her name on it and started painting. She was painting away when Josh questioned her, "What are you going to wrap in there, Kayla? You didn't make any ornaments." It was an innocent question, but Kayla started to wail, but this time, I saw tears.

She started screaming. "I don't know who I am going to give it to! I hate my mom, and I hate my dad. My dad wants us to come home because he made us a new house and wants us to be a family, but my mom doesn't want to be a family with him because she has a boyfriend, and my dad doesn't know about my mom's boyfriend, and I don't want my dad to kill my mom and her boyfriend, and so I don't even have a family, and I don't even want a stupid family!" The whole thing just erupted out of her. The whole class was stunned and stared at her, speechless.

She threw down her paintbrush and crawled under the table. She was sobbing, but this time, she was holding her head. She was rocking back and forth and whispering, "Oh no, oh no, oh no. You weren't supposed to tell. Stupid, stupid, you weren't supposed to tell." She kept saying it over and over again. I knew instantly that the long-held secret had finally spewed out. I let her calm down under the table while I tried to help the rest of my class. I knew she was tortured, but I knew she was safe.

Poor Josh. He didn't even know what happened. He ran over to her and knelt and was saying, "I'm sorry, Kayla. I'm so sorry." He had tears in his eyes and was stunned by her reaction.

I went over and knelt by Josh and rubbed his back. I took his hands in mine and looked him in the eye. I said, "Josh, this is not your fault. She is upset, but not at you. We know you didn't mean to hurt her feelings. She has a big problem in her life she is trying to work out. Thank you for caring about her. I'm going to try to help her, okay? This is not your fault." He was very upset by the whole situation but calmed down. He wanted to help but I wasn't even exactly sure what to do to help Kayla.

By now, Kayla had calmed herself down and was lying under the table, crying. I asked the kids to get back to work. I climbed under the table with her. She was a broken child. She was crying real, heartfelt tears. Her little heart was broken. I rubbed her back and tried to calmly talk to her. I could tell she was exhausted. Eventually, thankfully, she fell asleep.

I walked the other kids down to lunch and picked up a lunch for Kayla. I explained what had happened to the counselor and asked her to come in with me. When I returned to my room, Kayla was stirring. I told her that I had gotten her some lunch. She thanked me and crawled out from under the table. I handed her some tissues. Her face was swollen and her eyes were red, filled with pain.

I said, "You have been carrying a huge secret for a long time, and I think it's time for you to let us help. We care about you and want to help." She dissolved into tears again. She finally could tell us that she had accidently walked into the laundry room and saw her mom sitting on the washing machine and that her boyfriend from high school was standing between her legs and that he undid her bra and was kissing her and touching her. She said she didn't know if they saw her but that her dad was going to go crazy when he found out. She explained that her dad thinks that her mom and that guy were just friends, but she didn't think they were just friends anymore. She seemed distraught. She made us promise not to tell her dad.

I asked her when she had seen this happen, and she told us it was right before Halloween because she was going into the laundry room to get her witch's hat. I was amazed and hurt that she had been keeping this secret for nearly two months. She was tortured and broken-hearted and really scared about what her dad was going to do when he found out. Once again, she begged us not to tell anyone, especially her mom and dad. I held her in my lap and rocked her and tried to calm her.

Both the counselor and I explained that we cared about her and that we were concerned that she felt safe. The counselor explained that this was not her problem — that this was a grown-up problem and that she needed to only worry about kid problems. The counselor told her that Christmas was almost here and that that was what she needed to worry about. She asked if Kayla would come with her, and she told her that they were going to solve this problem so she could have a wonderful Christmas.

Our counselor is amazing with these little kids and their big problems.

They went to visit with the principal and called her mom and asked her to come to the school so they could work it all out. Kayla was very apprehensive about it, but the counselor promised her she would protect her and help her. She said that she knew her mom loved her and would feel sad that she had been so worried. I was so grateful that Kayla trusted this amazingly kind and loving counselor.

After they left, I quickly made two ornaments for Kayla, one for her dad and one for her mom, hoping this would help. When the kids came in from lunch recess, they asked about Kayla and really wanted to help. Josh finished painting her wrapping paper, and the other kids helped make a card for each of her parents. They wanted to talk about what Kayla had said. I told them that her parents were having some problems, but that our counselor was going to help her sort them out so that they could have a great Christmas. I really wanted to let the subject drop.

A few minutes later, I heard the kids start talking to each other. One of them said, "My dad has a girlfriend my mom doesn't know about." Another one said, "Mine, too. That is why my parents got divorced." Another one said, "I know how you feel. I have two moms and two dads because of it." I was shocked, but just listened to them, feeling so bad that this was a conversation that second graders could have. I think it helped them understand what Kayla was going through.

One of the kids said, "Now I understand about all of the drama

Kayla has. I feel so sorry for her!" I was amazed at their compassion. Even the kids with intact families were concerned.

Kayla's mom came to the school and met with the counselor, the principal, and Kayla, and they all discussed what had happened. Kayla's mom was humiliated, but tried hard to focus on what Kayla needed. She explained that they had had a really rough couple of months because she and her four girls had moved in with her sister and her husband and their babies. She explained that her high-school boyfriend had contacted her and that they had gotten together but that it was now over. She didn't know that Kayla had seen them and was mortified. She said that they were going to go back to Wyoming for Christmas and that she was going to try to put their family back together. Kayla's dad had hit her when he found out that the old boyfriend had contacted her, but since then, he had gotten some counseling and was ready to put their family back together, too. He had finished building their new home and had it decorated for Christmas, and they were leaving that day to go back.

Kayla's mom took her hands and looked her in the eyes and told her she was so sorry for all the things that had happened and that she wished she would have talked to her when she saw what she saw. She told her that she loved her dad and that she was going to try as hard as she could to put their family back together. The counselor told me that Kayla hugged her and said she was so happy because she wanted her family back.

Kayla skipped back into our room to pick up her stuff. She was happy and singing and smiling and thanked us for completing her gifts for her parents. She packed up her stuff and briefly told me that she was going back to Wyoming to see her dad and her new house and that she hoped I had a great Christmas, too. She said our counselor would tell me the rest. She smiled and ran out of the room to go home with her mom.

Kayla didn't return after Christmas. Her new school in Wyoming requested her records. I asked her new teacher how she was doing. She told me she was delightful and laughed a lot and was very chatty.

She told me she had not noticed any wailing. She said she was very smart and happy. When I asked about Kayla's family, she said that her dad brought her and her sisters to school every morning and that her mom picked them up after school. She said they were a great family. I was so relieved. I prayed that all the drama was gone and that she could be her happy, wonderful little self again.

23

ANGELYNN

Angelynn was an exceptionally beautiful child. She was Hispanic with huge onyx eyes and thick black hair. Her mother made sure her hair was always fixed beautifully, and she just had such an exquisite look about her. Despite being very pretty, she was very, very little. She had just turned 7, so she was one of the younger kids in the class, but even though she lacked in size, there was nothing small about her personality. She was such a kind and loving person to everyone, and she loved to laugh and have fun with the other students.

Early in the year, Angelynn explained to me that she was the assistant mom at her house. She had a brother named Dallas, who was in kindergarten. She also had a 4-year-old brother and a 2-year-old sister. She said they were very busy at their house. She told me that she liked it best when her dad had a job because he was really mean, especially when he didn't have a job.

It became evident very quickly that Angelynn was very afraid of her father. She confided in me that when he was drunk, he would get crazy mean. She told me that her mom would tell her to take all the little kids into the bathroom and to lock the door and watch them while she tried to calm her dad down when he was drunk.

Angelynn told me that she knows her dad hits her mom and makes her cry and makes her bleed. She said she worries a lot about her mom, but that it was really hard for her to keep both of the boys and the baby quiet when they were all in the bathroom for a long time. She said her dad hates it when anyone cries. She was very unemotional about it.

She told the story so matter-of-factly that it almost sounded like a daily occurrence. This seemed like a lot of pressure to put on a 7-year-old child. One day, Angelynn asked me what a "bastard baby was." It surprised me. I asked her where she had heard those words. She told me that her dad had yelled at her the night before and said that he didn't even know why he had to take care of her because she was someone else's bastard baby. He told her that he knew he had to take care of the other three kids but that he should just throw her out into the street. She told me he says stuff like that all of the time and that he just got fired again from his new job and so he gets drunk or high on drugs. She said her mom told her to ignore him and that he doesn't know what he is talking about.

We were working together in a learning station. There was Angelynn, four other children, and me. Angelynn went right on talking as she worked on her phonics activity. The other kids were working at first, but stopped to listen to her. She finally said, "I just don't know what a bastard baby is, so I was hoping you could tell me because you always tell us that we can ask you anything and that if you don't know then you would find out." I sat staring at her, stunned. I stumbled around with my words. I finally asked her to come talk to me in private, and we went over to my desk.

I took her hands in my hands and asked her to look me in the eyes. She did. I said, "Angelynn, I want you to listen closely to me. When your dad takes drugs or drinks alcohol, he does and says things he shouldn't. Drugs and alcohol make people's bodies do things that are bad. When your dad calls you that bad name, he is saying that you're not really his daughter, but I know that you're a remarkable young lady, and he should feel so very lucky to have you in his life. I think your dad is hurting because he lost another job, and sometimes, when people feel hurt, they want to hurt other people. So I want you to remember that when he says mean things it's the drugs and alcohol talking. I know this because I know you're an amazing little girl, and he should know it, too. She hugged me and smiled and said "Okay!" and ran back to the table to get to work. My heart hurt for her.

That afternoon, I called Angelynn's mom and talked to her about the situation. She was very hesitant to speak to me, and I got the sense that the dad was in the same room. I asked her if she would mind coming in and visiting with me when she had a minute so that I could get her help with Angelynn's "reading." We both knew I was masking my message, and she figured out that I knew what was going on.

A few days later, right before school started, I got a phone call. It was Angelynn's mom. She said her husband had gotten a job. He was starting that day, and she asked if she could come in and visit with me right after school. I said, "Yes, of course. Whenever you are free, please come in." She said okay and added that she would need to bring her other kids with her. I agreed. I kept Angelynn with me after school until her mother showed up.

When she walked in at 3:00 p.m., I was struck with how beautiful she was. Angelynn definitely took after her mother. She was a small woman with dark features and clear beautiful brown skin. Angelynn had her huge eyes. I noticed immediately that she was wearing an enormous amount of makeup and realized that she was probably covering up some bruises. She spoke very quickly and explained that her husband had already lost his new job and that he was parking the car outside, so she didn't have much time to talk to me. She said she appreciated all of the help I had been giving Angelynn and that she was glad Angelynn could confide in me, but that she needed me to not make any more problems because it made her husband very, very angry. She was apologetic, but I could tell she was terrified. Her other little kids were running around my room like they had just been set free from a zoo.

A few minutes later, her husband walked into the room. Everyone's behavior changed. The little kids got very quiet and came and sat on chairs. Angelynn's mom's whole body language changed. She became very withdrawn and quiet. Angelynn got as close as she possibly could to her mother. It seriously felt like a raging bull had just walked into a china store. There was tension in the room, and it was very uncomfortable. I tried to cover up any exchange her mother and I had just had. I acted like I was continuing with my sentence. I explained that it would be very helpful for Angelynn's reading if they could practice sight words every night, and I handed her a small pile of 3 x 5 flash cards with the sight words written on them. I could tell by the look in her eyes that she was very grateful I hadn't mentioned anything about what Angelynn had told me. I tried very hard to send her a message that she could trust me and that all I wanted was for everyone to be safe.

The husband finally said, "Are you done yet? Can we go?" I stood and stuck my hand out to shake his hand, but he turned and walked away.

Angelynn's mom took my hand and shook it. She looked me straight in the eye and said, "Thank you. We truly appreciate your help!" When he got to the door, Angelynn's father turned and said to me, "Just so you know, I believe it's your job to teach the little sh** to read at school, and we will take care of her at home, so I would appreciate it if you would mind your own f****** business!" He picked up the youngest girl roughly and stormed out of the room.

Angelynn took the youngest brother's hand, the mom grabbed Dallas' hand, and they all followed him out of my classroom. As she left, Angelynn's mom turned to me and mouthed the words, "I am so sorry!" Then they were all gone.

I knew at that moment that my purpose was to do everything I could to help Angelynn feel safe and loved and cared for at school. I now understood how important it was to be consistent and available when she needed to talk. I knew that setting boundaries for myself would save trouble for Angelynn and her mom. I really wanted to tell that dad off. I wanted to tell him that he had an amazing daughter and that he should treasure her and that he was lucky to have her in his life. But after the visit, I knew better. I hoped that I had conveyed to the mom that I cared about Angelynn and was willing to do what I could to help her. I was scared for them all and knew I needed to do whatever I could to not make things worse for them.

Over the next several months, Angelynn confided more and more information to me. I gave her my cell number and told her that if she ever needed me I would come to her house and help her or I would call the police or do whatever she needed. She seemed to treasure that little piece of paper and told me she hid it in a special place and that she was going to call me if she couldn't stand it anymore. I told her how incredibly brave she was and how much I loved being her teacher. She said she loved being at school because everyone was happy and safe there. I worried so much about that little girl and got a sick feeling every time I put her on the bus to go home to that father.

Of course, I let the principal and the counselor know of the situation. The dad had stated that, under no uncertain terms, either Angelynn or Dallas were allowed to visit with anyone in the school, especially the counselor, or he would sue the school and the school district.

The principal kept in close contact with the police department. Knowing that they had a long rap sheet on her father and wanting to do anything and everything they could to keep the children safe, they were prepared to intervene and arrest him at any given time if needed. The principal made sure that we checked on Angelynn and Dallas to make sure they never had any bruises or scrapes or showed any signs of abuse.

I made sure that I always had an open-door policy with Angelynn. She knew she could come and talk to me anytime she needed to. There were a few times when she asked to miss library or music or recess to visit with me. I always tried to stay calm and just listen to her. She was so worried about her mom. She did tell me that her dad never hit the kids, but if they were naughty, then their dad would scream at their mom and hit her and yell at her about raising little brats. Angelynn explained that they were afraid all the time.

Angelynn confided in me that they didn't have any food in their home. I sent home the paperwork to have them put on the free or reduced lunch schedule, but her dad tore up the paper. We all worked together with food services and made sure they ate breakfast and lunch at school.

I was also able to get them on the backpack program. This is a program that works through the food bank. Each Friday, our school social worker picks up bags of food for the kids that need food from the food bank. We put the food in their backpacks, and it feeds them all weekend. At first, Angelynn said her dad had a fit because they didn't need help from that stupid school, but then she said he mellowed and let them eat the food, which helped their home situation a lot.

One of the most interesting things about Angelynn was how grateful she was for everything. She always thanked me for my kindness and for caring about her. She let me know how much she appreciated the food and that she loved the way I made sure she and Dallas always had something to eat. I was in awe of her graciousness and appreciation. She would go out of her way to make sure that all the kids in our class were okay.

In this kind of situation, many children of abuse become very self-focused. Angelynn didn't. I think her situation made her more compassionate and empathetic toward others. We had many talks about the concern she had for some specific students in our class. She was a remarkable young lady.

Academically, she was struggling. I noticed that, when it came to completing school work, she would just stare off into the distance. I would work with her individually as much as I possibly could, but she really struggled to focus. Her reading did improve, however. I made sure she had a reading buddy and a learning friend. I made sure she got extra help in the reading classes and made sure she knew when she had little successes. I think she had so many worries that focusing on school exhausted her.

There were several times when the kindergarten teacher would appear in my classroom and ask if she could borrow Angelynn for a minute, as they needed her to help calm Dallas down. He had begun acting up and hurting other kids. They didn't want to call home because they knew it would make things worse for him. Angelynn would patiently go into the kindergarten class and take Dallas out in the hall and talk to him. She told me that she would say to him, "Dallas, you have a choice. You can choose to behave and make good choices or we are going to have to call dad, and he will help you make good choices. So, what's it going to be?" She said she told him that if he would straighten up she wouldn't tell dad about the problems he had caused. She said he usually straightened up. If I hadn't known better, I would have sworn there was a tiny grown-up living inside that beautiful little girl.

Toward the end of the school year, Angelynn told me that her dad had gotten a job in the oil fields in South Dakota. She was thrilled because he couldn't get good jobs anywhere because he had a felony on his record and that this could be a good job for him. (I thought it was so sad that a second grader even knew what a felony on their record meant.) Anyway, they were all excited and were praying that he would actually go and work hard. She seemed so relieved and hoped they would have a good, peaceful summer.

She told me she was worried about Dallas because he was "out of control," but that she was going to try to help her mom with him and her younger siblings, too. I was continually amazed by this beautiful little girl. She had a heart of gold. I told her that she could call me in the summer if she ever needed me, and I made her promise to come back and see me when she was in third grade. I let her know that she was a precious light in my life and had such power to do good for people. I thanked her for her strength and her bravery, the whole time thinking, *No child should ever have to be that brave*. She was a remarkable little girl.

24

DALLAS

The close relationship I had with Angelynn continued when she went to third grade. Several times a month, she would come in and ask if she could have lunch with me. We visited a lot about the situation her family was in. She told me that her mom had kicked her dad out of the house, but that he won't leave them alone. She told me that life was happier when it was just their mom and the kids. Angelynn was really worried that her dad was going to do something bad. Her mom was trying to work with a lawyer, but her dad was not willing to work with them because he doesn't want the divorce.

Angelynn was excited that her little brother Dallas was going to be in my class the next year. Angelynn would be in the fourth grade while Dallas was in second. She told me that he was a little pill, but she told him he had to be nice to me because I could help him a lot. She told me that I might need her help with him and that she was willing to come whenever I needed her. She was a gem.

Dallas was a tiny little guy. He was built like a gymnast: small, but powerful. Like Angelynn, he was a beautiful child. He had clear, brown skin with big, dark-brown eyes, black hair, and a delightful smile. I liked him instantly. The first thing he said to me was, "So what's up, Teach? My sister Angelynn says you are the coolest teacher ever and that I gotta be nice to you. So let's get busy."

Dallas loved to giggle. He had such a fun personality. We hit it off immediately. We would joke around with each other. He was a real bright light in our classroom. He would tell me that he got to see "Good Dad" on weekends and that he would take him to the park and they would have fun. He said that sometimes he even took him and his siblings to McDonald's and that it was his favorite. He loved hanging out with Good Dad. I could always tell when he had spent time with "good dad" because he was really chatty and funny and happy.

One Monday, he came into the classroom, hung up his backpack, and slammed himself down into his chair. I hadn't seen this behavior before. When I said "Good morning" to him, he actually growled at me. He seemed very angry. I asked him to come over and visit with me. As he walked over, he knocked everything off the tables and knocked down chairs and dumped out a cup of pencils. I said, "Wowzers, Dallas, it looks like you had a tough weekend. Do you want to tell me about it?"

He unleashed a tirade, "Yeah, Miss Melanie. Bad Dad showed up this weekend, and he is a big fat asshole. I hate that guy. Angelynn had to lock us in the bathroom again. We could hear him yelling and breaking stuff. My mom called the police. He is not even supposed to be at our house. I hate 'bad dad' so much. The police took him away."

I listened to him carefully. When he finished, I said, "Wowzers, Dallas, I am so sorry that happened. I can see it made you very angry. How can I help?"

He had no idea. I checked with our school counselor, and she let him come to her office and punch the punching bag for a while. She also gave him a stress ball. This seemed to help, and he calmed down a little.

The thing I noticed was that Dallas started getting pretty violent with the other kids. They would tell me that he pushed them or that he would punch them and run away. I had Dallas stay in with me during recess, and we visited about the issue. He told me that he couldn't help himself. I explained to him that I cared a lot about him, but that I couldn't let him hurt the other kids. I said to him, "Hey, little buddy, when you make choices like that, you take my choices away. I must give you a 'red ticket' and report you to the principal. That's my job. I can't let you hurt people. So let's make a plan. What can we do to keep you from hurting other kids?"

He told me he didn't want to hurt other kids, but they made him so mad, and he didn't know what to do with his "madness." I felt so bad for him. He was tortured. The plan we came up with was taking deep breaths, counting to ten, squeezing his stress ball, and running around the playground. We tried everything we could think of.

Mom had kicked Dad out of the house and was now seeing another man, who was a former boyfriend. Dallas really liked the "new guy" and said things were "pretty calmer" for his mom. Dad was still in the picture, though, and hated the new guy. Real Dad picked the kids up every weekend to spend a little time with them.

Each Monday, Dallas would come in and tell us whom he got to spend the weekend with. It was either Good Dad or Bad Dad. His behavior seemed to line up with whichever dad he went with. When I asked Angelynn about what was going on, she explained that Good Dad and Bad Dad were the same person. Oh my goodness, did that ever surprise me. I thought he was talking about the new guy as the "good dad," but when I asked him about it, he explained that he never knows which "real dad" would show up: Good Dad or Bad Dad. I thought Dad must have had a split personality because Dallas described the behavior between the two dads so differently. I was honestly surprised that they were the same man.

Angelynn explained that their dad had fought to get visitation rights with them. Then he would come to their house and, depending if he had been drinking or not, would determine if he was Good Dad or Bad Dad. If he had been drinking, their mom didn't want him to take them, and then they would get into a huge fight, and then he would hit her and she would call the police again and she, Angelynn, would take the kids into the bathroom until the police got there. She said that their dad couldn't control his temper, so she understood why Dallas couldn't either.

Eventually, Dallas wasn't able to go to recess at all anymore because he hurt too many kids. He would stay in with me or go with our behavior tech. We would have long talks about what kind of man he wanted to grow up to be. I would ask him, "Do you want to be Good Man or Bad Man? You see what Bad Man does to other people, so what do you think?"

He would say he wanted to be Good Man, but that, sometimes, Bad Man would just take over. For some reason, he wanted to please me because I told him that I would keep him safe but that I had to keep the other kids safe, too. He seemed to understand, so he kept himself under control in the classroom as long as he knew exactly what we were going to do. If anything changed or our schedule got messed up, he would lose his temper. I watched this very closely so I could warn him. If we were going to have a fire drill or go to an assembly or anything out of the normal schedule, I would let him know, and he would get mad, but then he would just adjust.

One of the things that we enjoy in my classroom is when the kids sing while I play the guitar. We sing some crazy, funny songs. Dallas really liked singing the funny songs and would over-laugh at them. Sometimes, I seriously thought he was bipolar because he would go from laughing like a crazy person to angry and then depressed in less than an hour.

Every week, the kids get to do Show-and-Tell. I ended up having to talk to Dallas before he did a Show-and-Tell because he would tell us things that were not really appropriate for second graders to hear. He knew a lot about violence and had some gruesome stories to tell. I told him that the kids and I couldn't handle his gross, graphic stories. He was sad, but he understood.

One Wednesday, Dallas asked me if he could borrow my guitar to sing a song he had written for Show-and-Tell. I was so excited that he was using his talent for singing, and I thought maybe a star would be born. I helped him put the guitar strap around his neck and handed him my pick. He explained to the kids that he had written a song for them. He started to strum the guitar. He had no idea what he was doing, and the guitar was huge compared to him, but he sounded like a little country singer. These are the words he sang:

"Oh man, I miss my dog because now my dog is dead.

My dad got mad at my brother and me and shot him in the head.

We forgot to pick up our dog's poop, so my dad went and got his gun.

I got blood and brains all over my face, and so now we don't have fun."

Horrified was the best word I could use to describe mine and everyone else's reaction. Dallas kept on strumming the guitar until I stopped him and said, "That is the saddest song I've ever heard," hoping it was something he made up and not wanting to know if he hadn't. I asked the kids to thank Dallas and then hurried to the next Show-and-Tell.

Angelynn confirmed that that had actually happened when Dallas was in first grade. She said it was a big mess and took them forever to clean it up. She said Dallas wasn't able to sleep for weeks after it happened. She also told me that their dad got into huge trouble for "discharging a firearm within city limits" and that he had been arrested, but the judge just took away his gun and let him go. She said that it didn't matter what he did because the judge would just let him go.

Dallas and Angelynn both missed several days of school right after Thanksgiving. I was very concerned and was unable to get in touch with their mother because her phone had been disconnected. When Dallas came back to school, he was out of control. He refused to work and was shouting at everyone and was really mean if anyone even tried to talk to him. I was stunned and asked the kids to give him some space. He wouldn't talk to me and just screamed, "Leave me alone!"

I sent a message to Angelynn's teacher, asking if she could

come and visit with me during lunchtime. I kept Dallas with me because I thought he would hurt someone if I let him go to the lunchroom. I took him to the counselor's office so he could punch the punching bag. When Angelynn got to my room, I asked her what had happened. She told me that it was really bad. She said they had gone to their aunt's house (their mother's sister) for Thanksgiving. After dinner, their dad showed up and started screaming at their mom. He grabbed her by her hair and pushed her into his truck and drove away. Their aunt called the police, but they couldn't find them. She went on to tell me that their dad had taken their mom somewhere and beat her up and raped her and tore her clothes and that she was a mess. She said some neighbors found her and called the police, and they took her to the hospital, but their dad ran away, and the police couldn't find him.

Their mom had been in the hospital for a few days, and she had filed charges against their dad. They had to stay with their aunt until she could come get them. She had picked them up the night before, and that was why they were at school that day.

She also told me that their mom had gotten a job, but that she had to miss a few days because their dad hurt her so badly. She had to go back to work that day, so they were all going to stay at their aunt's house until the police found their dad. She was so matter-of-fact about the whole story, and I was horrified. She told me that Dallas was so angry and confused that he didn't know what to do with himself. I made sure that she visited with the counselor, too. It was a mess.

When I talked to Dallas and told him that I knew about what happened, he broke down and cried. I took him into my arms and rocked him and told him how sorry I was. He sobbed and sobbed. He finally calmed down enough to talk to me. He said he was really scared for his mom and that he was also really scared for his dad because he thought the police were going to kill him, and if they didn't, the judge was going to let him go, and then he was going to come back and hurt his mom again. I rocked him and kept saying,

"You're safe now. It's okay. You're safe now." I seriously didn't know what to do or say.

I tried to call and talk to the mom, but Angelynn told me that their dad had smashed her phone and that she couldn't afford to get another one. Our school's social worker stepped in and got her a new phone. I was relieved to find out that all the kids and their mom were staying with their aunt and uncle until the dad was caught.

Before Dallas left on Friday afternoon, I tried to reassure him that his aunt and uncle were going to keep him safe. He said he didn't believe me, and I had to agree: I didn't believe me either. I hugged him and was terrified to send him home. The mom picked them up from school that day. She still had bruises on her face, and her arm was wrapped. My heart broke for her.

The next day, the Saturday evening local news told a terrifying story. They reported that early that morning a man showed up at his ex-wife's job at a local assisted-living center. He pointed a gun at his ex-wife's face and tried to force her to leave with him. She refused. Her boss, who had heard the argument, called the police. When the gunman heard the approaching sirens, he fled. The ex-wife described his truck, and they were able to track him as he was fleeing. They chased him for several miles and had to force him off the road. He still refused to get out of the truck, so they used tear gas to get him to surrender. When they took him into custody, the police were unable to find the gun. The wife was unhurt, but she had been taken into protective custody until her ex-husband was apprehended and booked.

When I heard his name, and saw the mug shot, I knew it was Angelynn and Dallas' dad. As much as I hate that another woman was so horribly treated by him, I was relieved that the police knew where he was. The news had reported that he was being charged with kidnapping, rape, attempted murder, and fleeing the scene of a crime. They were searching for the gun and would charge him with a gun crime as soon as it was located. I was praying that he would be sent to prison for a very long time. Now, I was hoping I could help Dallas.

All the children came to school on Monday. Angelynn came to see me at recess and told me that their mom was pretty shook up, but that she was going to be okay and that she didn't lose her job and that her boss was going to try to help her. She seemed so relieved and hopeful. I was happy to see her smile again. She said they had moved back into their house and that their mom's attorney said that their dad was going to be in jail for a very long time.

Dallas, however, was a completely different story. He came in angry and was out of control. I talked to him and tried to calm him down. The counselor tried to talk to him, but he was uncontrollable. His mom had to come and pick him up. They spent the day together, and she tried to let him know that she was okay. We fought this problem all week. He was a wreck. He refused to do any work and was completely in his own little world. His mom and I tried to figure out how to help him. She picked him up every day because he refused to do any work and was hurting the other kids. He was so disruptive that he was hurting everyone else's learning, too.

We only had a few weeks until Christmas break. I considered having him stay home until after Christmas because he was doing nothing constructive at school. I thought a lot and prayed a lot and finally had an idea. I called his mom and asked her if she could bring him to school early on Monday so we could have a talk.

When they got there, I asked them to sit down. I asked Dallas if the reason he was acting so crazy was because he was worried about his mom. He yelled at me, "Yes, Miss Melanie, I am the man of the house now, and I am responsible to take care of my mom. How can I do that when I am at school? What if my dad escapes from jail and kills her? He told me he was going to kill her or die trying. I can't protect her when I am at school. What do you want me to do?" By now, he was crying. His mom and I looked at each other. We both had tears in our eyes. Poor little guy. He was in so much pain and despair.

I said to him, "Okay, Dallas, I am super impressed that you are the man of the house now. It's amazing that you want to take such good care of your mom. I think your mom really wants you to learn to read and to work hard at school." His mom confirmed my words.

I continued. "I have a plan. How about this: anytime during the day that you get worried about your mom, I'll give you the phone pass, and you can go to the office and call her and make sure she is okay. Do you think that would help?"

She clapped her hands and said, "Dallas, that would be a wonderful idea. Then you'll know I'm safe, and I'll know you're working hard at school. It's perfect! What do you think?"

We could tell he was thinking about it. After several minutes, he asked, "So, I can call whenever I want to make sure she is okay?"

I said, "Yup, anytime you're worried about her, but then you have to promise to get your work done. Can we shake on it?"

He actually smiled and said "Okay!"

His mom thanked me repeatedly. I told her that it was really important that she answer her phone when he called. She assured me that she would.

The first day, he called six or seven times, and every time he called his mom, she told him she was doing well and that she was excited to see what work he had done that day. As time went on, he called less and less. He would just walk up to me and touch my arm. I would look at him. He would say "Please," I would nod, and he would go call. When he came back, he was so much calmer and would get right to work.

On the Friday before Christmas, he asked if he could eat lunch with me. I told him how impressed and proud of him I was. I told him that he was going to turn out to be Good Man after all. He shook his head and said, "No, I'm not!" I was shocked.

"What? I love how you watch out for your mom and your sisters and brother, and you're working hard at school and getting your work done. You're doing great!"

He put his head down on the desk. I waited. He finally said, "Teacher, I know something I'm not supposed to know."

I asked, “Is it something I can help you with?”

He sat for a long time and stared at his food. He finally whispered, “I’m not supposed to tell anyone ever, but ... I ... I ... I know where the gun is.” He looked at me with tears in his eyes. I didn’t know what to say, so I just sat there and stared at him. There was another long silence. I waited.

Finally, he said, “My dad threw the gun into the bushes when he left my mom’s work, and his mom went and got it out of the bushes, and she has it now.” He just sat there and stared.

I rubbed his back and whispered, “Dallas, we have to tell the police. If they can find the gun, then he will have to stay in jail longer, and he won’t get out and hurt you or your mom.”

He said, “I know.”

Then he put his head down on my lap and wept. I called his mom, and she came and got him and took him to the police station. They called him a miniature hero, which he told us about in Show-and-Tell. I told him to write a song about it.

They were able to recover the gun, which made the dad’s sentence much longer because the crime became a gun crime. Dallas was devastated because he loved Good Dad, but he was torn apart because he hated Bad Dad so much. I knew he had years and years of work ahead of him to get all the way through the nightmare he had experience and try and figure out which kind of man he would be. I still pray for him and his family. They moved out of our school boundaries at the end of that year, so I have had a hard time keeping track of the family. Last thing I heard was that Dallas was in the alternate school because he kept hurting people. I pray with all my heart that someday Good Man will take over that little guy. He has so much potential.

25

TRAVIS

One Thursday, I called on Travis to do his Show-and-Tell. Travis was an adorable little tow-headed, blue-eyed fellow. He had lost his front teeth and would always smile the cheesiest smile.

He got up and showed us a plastic bracelet. It was about two centimeters wide and looked like it had a piece of paper in it. He showed us that it did have a label on it. He said, "This is the bracelet my little brother Treagen weared this summer when he had to go to the hospital to get his weed whacker fixed." The kids all turned and looked at me to see if I understood what he was talking about, but I didn't understand either.

I said, "That is interesting, Travis, but we don't actually understand what you're talking about. Can you please explain it to us?"

He took a deep breath and said, "Okay. This summer, when it was really hot, we were playing in our little swimming pool on our driveway, and my baby brother, who was 19 months old, was all wet and playing in the water. My mom was pulling weeds. My little brother taked off his diaper. He climbed onto our little plastic trike, but the seat was broken, and it cut his private parts — you know — his weed whacker, and he bleeded all over the place, and my mom had to hold him all of the way to the hospital because it was bleeding and bleeding. She had to rush us to the hospital and hold his weed whacker at the same time, and the doctor had to do surgery and fix his little weed whacker. And this is the bracelet that he wore so we would know which one of the kids at the hospital was him. The end!"

We all just kind of stared at him, speechless! There was a long silence when, finally, a little boy named Tyson blurted out, "Do you mean he got his pee-pee caught in the trike, and the doctor had to put stitches in it?"

Travis replied, "Yup! That is exactly what I mean. My little brother almost gotted his weed whacker cut off, so he had to wear this bracelet at the hospital so they knew we could take him home."

Still shocked, I stumbled around with my words a little. "Um, um, well, um, who can tell us what kind of learning Travis' Show-and-Tell is?"

Hesitantly Tyson said, "Social studies, because he went to the hospital." Another child said, "Science, because they had to know how to work on his little body and his boy parts." Then there was a long, long pause, and finally, another little boy said, questioningly, "Math? Because they had to measure how long to make the stitches to fix his weed whacker?"

I laughed out loud at how concerned all of the kids were about the seriousness of Travis' little brother's tricycle accident. Every day, several kids would ask him how his brother's little weed whacker was doing. Every day, he gave the same answer. "I don't know. He won't let me see the little weed whacker, but my mom puts medicine on it, so I think it's doing good!"

26

MARLYNN

MarLynn had a beautiful, angel face. She had big blue eyes, full pink lips, and long blonde hair. Sometimes her hair was fixed really cute, and sometimes it was a mess. Sometimes she was dressed like a little fashion model, and sometimes she was filthy. She had a cute little personality but got quite emotional if things didn't go her way. She would start screaming like the world was ending. I would describe her life as high drama.

Her first-grade teacher told me that she had spent several weeks in a mental institution and that a psychiatrist was working with her. I asked if I needed to visit with her psychiatrist, but she told me that I was supposed to treat her like I would treat any other child. "Great," I said, and we started the year.

Immediately, I knew I needed to start building a relationship with her. I noticed that she responded amazingly to positive reinforcement. I made sure that I said at least three positive things to her during the morning. She would keep working hard if any praise was attached. She was a beginning reader and pretty slow. She was working with the resource room teacher on reading fundamentals because she had missed so much school the year before. I noticed the drama lessened if I thanked her for working hard

The thing about MarLynn that stumped me was her look. Somedays, she was so clean and adorable, and some days, she was a mess and looked like a little uncared-for ragamuffin. When I asked her about it, she told me that sometimes when her mother tries to comb her hair or wash her face she screams at her, but then sometimes she likes it when her mom takes care of her. I asked her how she thinks her mom feels about that. She said that her mom gets really, really frustrated with her and mad when she won't let her help her look cute. MarLynn stomped her foot and said, "Sometimes I just don't want to look cute, okay? What's the big deal?"

Every day was a new adventure with MarLynn. We never knew what kind of mood she would be in. Some days, she worked hard, and some days she cried all day. I paid close attention to her mood. If I could tell she was just whining, I would say, "Hey, my little friend MarLynn. The whining isn't actually working for me, so I need you to think of another way to communicate."

Most of the time, she would say, "Okay!" and then get back to work. Occasionally, that would set her off, and she would start screaming. I would quietly ask her to go out in the hall between the two outside doors and scream, but that when she was finished, she was welcome to come back to class. She would, and a few minutes later, she would come back and be fine. Sometimes I could tell she just needed to talk, so when I got a chance, I would pull her aside and visit with her.

She would tell me about the drama in her life. She and her mom lived together, and occasionally, she would see her dad, but not very often. She said her grandma was nice to her, but her mom and her grandma fought a lot. She lived a highly emotional life.

One morning, she ran into our room shortly after the bell rang, and she was mad. She chucked her backpack on the floor and threw her chair off of the desk, where she had placed it the night before. She didn't even sit down. She walked to the corner, folded her arms, and pouted. It was easy to tell she was upset and on the verge of a meltdown. She was very unkempt. Her hair was all over the place, her shoes didn't match, her clothes were dirty, and her face had food on it. She was a mess! I could tell she had a story to tell.

I whispered to her that I needed to get the other kids working on an activity and then I would visit with her. That seemed to calm her down. She went over to my desk and paced back and forth until I was able to come over and talk with her.

When I came to her, she cuddled up to me. She laid her head on my shoulder and started to cry. I rubbed her back and rocked her for a while. She finally started to explain that she had had a "terrible, horrible" morning. She said she got up all by herself and went to her mom's bedroom to ask her to help her get ready for school.

She looked at me with those big, blue, tear-filled eyes and blurted, "There was a stranger man in her bed!" She put her head back on my shoulder and cried again. I was surprised, but I just held and rocked her.

Finally, she said, "I asked my mommy to help me get ready for school, and she just yelled at me and said, 'Just go get on the damn bus!' I told her I needed clean clothes and that I wanted her to fix my hair and help me brush my teeth and get some breakfast, but she just yelled, "Go get on the G**damned bus. I mean it! Now!"

She sobbed and sobbed. My heart broke for her. She told me that the man didn't have any clothes on and that he had a tattoo of a dragon on his arm. She said her mom made her feel really, really bad, and she didn't want to ever go home. She even asked me if she could come live with me. I handed her a tissue and continued to rock her and stroke her hair. She was so sad. I had not seen her like this before. She was very dramatic and did a lot of wailing and pretending to cry, but this was different. This little girl was heartbroken.

After several minutes, as the other children were finishing their work, I said to MarLynn, "Sweetie, I am truly sorry that this happened to you this morning. I can tell you have had a terrible, horrible day so far. I'm sure your mommy was tired, but she should have been kinder to you and helped you. But good news: I bet I can help you now. Would you like that?" She nodded and wiped her eyes and nose.

I said, "I have a brush and comb right here in my desk. Let's get it out and comb your beautiful hair, okay?" She nodded.

While I was combing her hair, I asked her how else I could help her. She said she didn't get to brush her teeth and that her clothes were the same ones she wore the day before and she was super hungry. I told her that I had a brand-new toothbrush and some toothpaste right here.

"Why don't you go in and brush your teeth? I will ask Miss Allison (our school social worker) to help you find some clean clothes and get you some breakfast." I could tell by the look on her face how grateful she was. She hugged me. I asked her if she felt better. She said "Yes, and thank you, Teacher!"

As she climbed off my lap, she turned around and moved her finger to indicate she wanted to whisper in my ear. I bent over to be able to hear her. She whispered, "Do you want to know the worst part about the whole morning?"

I smiled at her and said, "Of course, because now it's getting better."

She continued, "It was really bad ... because ... I saw ... my mommy's boobies! I never want to see those things again as long as I live!" I couldn't help it, I laughed out loud. Thank goodness MarLynn laughed too.

I sent her to brush her teeth. Our community services resource leader brought her some clean clothes and took her to eat breakfast. When she returned, things were much better. She ended up having a good day. I think she felt like she had bonded with me and was able to trust me and knew that I would help her. After that, we had a great relationship. She shared the things that happened during her life. She came to me when she was troubled, but the rest of the time, she was a pretty happy-go-lucky little, delightful lady. Sometimes I just felt so sad for her. She had a tough little life, but she learned a lot and started reading and became a pretty good student.

The summer after MarLynn left my class, her grandmother

called me and asked me to talk to MarLynn and see if I could calm her down. She said they had had a really tough summer, as MarLynn had gone back to the behavior that her family was calling a mental illness. They weren't sure what to do with her and didn't know how to help her. I was completely surprised that this was the same little girl. I told her grandma how sorry I was and how I would do anything I could to help. She said MarLynn was having a fit and that they would call me back when they calmed her down. I told her I'd love to visit with her. I waited and waited, but she never called me back. I have since tried to contact them, but I've yet to be able to make contact.

27

GARRETT

Music is an important part of my curriculum. The kids and I sing every day. I explain how important math is in music and teach them about rhythm, timing, and keeping a beat. It's also a great way to teach days of the week, months of the year, short vowels, long vowels, counting money, etc. The list goes go and on.

One day, while we were working on a patterning project, I put on KIDZ BOP. I explained that the song had four beats per measure and that it was a pattern like the ones we were making. They were working and dancing around. It was so fun to listen to them count to the beats.

While the kids were working and dancing, one of my boys came up to me, and we had a very interesting conversation:

Garrett: "Teacher, I love music, but playing Taylor Swift? Really?"

Teacher: "I like Taylor Swift, and it has a great beat. Most kids like Taylor Swift. What music do you like to listen to?"

Garrett: "I like the classics like The Walrus!"

Teacher: "Oh my goodness, I love The Beatles. How do you know The Beatles?"

Garrett: "I told you. I love all the classics."

Teacher: "That is awesome. Who else do you like?"

Garrett: "Well, I like ACDC and the Beach Boys and Billy Joel and The Rolling Stones. I like all the old stuff."

Teacher: "Garrett, I am very impressed with your choice of music. You have awesome taste. I love the classics, too."

Garrett: "Yeah, my family and I really like almost all the classics. I like The Beatles the most, and I like Michael Jackson. Oh, oh, oh! And I love anything done by SpongeBob."

Teacher: (Laughing) "Oh, SpongeBob. Is he a classic, too?"

Garrett: "Oh, yes, because SpongeBob sings all the classics. The other guys just sing their own songs. He is a really talented sponge, you know."

Teacher: "No, I actually hadn't realized that SpongeBob was a talented musician. Thanks for telling me about him."

Garrett: "Sure thing, Teacher. Hey, maybe someday Taylor Swift will be a classic like SpongeBob. Maybe she could sing some of his songs. Then I would probably like her."

Teacher: "I'll bet Taylor Swift is probably hoping for that, too!"

Garrett: "Yeah, probably. All the great ones do!"

28

AMANDA

In my whole career, I have never been able to retain a child in second grade because it's a held belief that it does more damage to a child to hold him/her back rather than it is to pass them to a higher grade, even if they are unprepared to move on. I usually saw the justification for this belief until I met Amanda.

Her mom brought her in to meet me on the first day of school. She was a little mop-topped, brown-eyed, brown-haired, adorable child. She had thick glasses and the thickest hair I have ever seen, and she talked all the time. I noticed immediately that she acted much younger than the rest of the kids. Her mom seemed frustrated with her and was thrilled that she got to leave her at school for six hours a day. She explained, "I need a break. She exhausts me. Good luck!" She almost ran out of my room.

I turned to talk to Amanda. She had crawled under the table and was growling. I knelt to see her face and try to make a connection with her. She growled at me and then snarled, "My dad is a wolf, and he came to see me last night." Wowzers! I was so surprised I wasn't sure what to say. Then she started to howl. I waited for a few minutes as she was anxiously engaged in her howling fantasy. She finally said, "I howl back at my dad so he knows I can hear him!"

The other kids were coming into the class now, as the bell had rung. My first thought was, *Welcome to the first day of school. It's going to be an interesting, crazy year.*

I said to Amanda, "Hey, buddy, how about if we start class, and maybe you can howl at your dad later when we have gotten our work done?"

She said, "Okay," and crawled out from under the table and sat in a chair. She seemed to assimilate pretty well at first. We played some get-to-know-you games, and when I introduced her to everyone, she said, "My dad is a wolf, and this is how I talk to him."

She proceeded to howl.

She then went on to tell us her name and that she lived with her mom and sometimes her grandma when her mom gets too mad at her. She said she just moved to Pocatello because her mom doesn't want her grandma to take her anymore because her grandma is taking care of too many kids.

The kids seemed to accept her explanation of her life and didn't even ask any questions. We went on to do our normal first-of-the-year activities. I have a little finger puppet show that I use to teach the kids the rules. Amanda listened with the rest of the children, although she did ask me why I didn't have a wolf puppet. She seemed like a happy, matter-of-fact kid who truly believed her dad was a wolf. I thought, *This little girl has quite a story to tell.*

A few days later, when it was her turn to pass out snack, she stayed in from recess to do so. I asked her to tell me about her dad, the wolf. She explained that her dad got killed in a car crash when he had a seizure or was drunk driving and his car hit a telephone pole and she was holding his head, and then his body died, but his spirit went into a wolf that was watching the accident. She said that the police told her that they saw a wolf run away from the accident and then howl to tell them to tell her that he always loved her and that he was going to watch out for her and that he made sure she was always safe. It was an amazing story, and she believed it with all her heart. I questioned her about holding his head when he died.

She said told me that it had happened but that she was pretty little, so she didn't remember it all.

I thought about her explanation for a while and then told her how lucky she was to have someone who cared about her so much and was watching out for her. I said he must be very proud of how hard she was working in school. She said she tells him every night about her day, and then she howls goodnight to him. Then she howled for me. Wowzers! What a story.

When her mom picked her up that day, I asked her about the wolf thing and the accident. Her mom told me that Amanda wasn't at the accident, but that her dad had died in a car crash when he hit a telephone pole. She said the police said he was on drugs, but she says he had a seizure and that they were still fighting about it. She told me that Amanda's grandma was taking care of her sister's and brother's children and that she couldn't handle them all, so she had moved away for a new start.

She told me that, in California, children could start kindergarten when they were 4 years old. Amanda's birthday was at the beginning of September and that she had lied about the year she was born, so she had started when she was 3. She told me that she was still only 5 years old but that she would be six in September. Everything made so much more sense now. It was obvious that she was much younger than the rest of the kids, who were 7 and would turn 8 during the school year.

Her mom explained to me that Amanda was a hard baby and that after her father died, she couldn't stand her anymore and could barely take care of her, so she had lied and put her in school so they could help her babysit. She was a tall girl, so it didn't surprise me that she had been able to get away with the deception.

Unfortunately, Amanda didn't know the alphabet or how to count to ten or how to hold a pencil or pretty much anything she needed to be successful in second grade.

As the school year went on, she got further and further behind because she wasn't really interested in learning. She really enjoyed her fantasy world of hiding under the tables and desks and howling and growling to her dad. I talked to the other kids and explained the situation. At first, they were annoyed, but they tried to understand. They would ask me, "Why is she so weird?" We spent a lot of time learning about the difference between fantasy and reality in books. I told them we have an example of fantasy versus reality right in our own classroom. Aren't we lucky? Amanda and I explained to the other kids what had happened to her dad and that she believed she could communicate with him if she became an animal. The kids thought it was cool.

Eventually, the kids asked Amanda to howl "hello" to her dad from them, which she gladly did. We did try to "train" her to only growl and howl during certain times of the day because it hurt the other kids' learning, and sometimes, it made it hard for me to teach. Sometimes she forgot, but she usually tried to oblige. I was able to get help from the resource room teacher, but it was a really tough year for everyone because it was so evident how far behind Amanda was.

She was usually a pretty happy-go-lucky kid who loved to laugh and giggle, especially during transition times. She started to turn into different animals to get to places. For instance, when she had to change stations, she would hop like a bunny. When she went to the restroom, she would crawl like a turtle. She loved her world of animal imagination.

One day, I noticed that she was very sad, and I could tell her face was tear stained. I smiled at her, but she just turned away. When we gathered for Sharing Circle, she sat on her knees. I asked her to please sit crisscross applesauce (on her bottom, cross-legged), but she said she couldn't. She acted like her bottom hurt. I let her sit how she could. During recess, I asked her to come and talk to me.

She explained that she had big sores on her bum and legs because her mom's new boyfriend beated her with his belt, so she couldn't sit down because it stinged her. My eyes teared up, and I opened my arms. She ran into my arms, and we cried together.

I was stunned. She told me that her mom spanked her all the time, but that her mom's new boyfriend named Jerry spanked her with a belt and that the buckle "hitted her bummy." She said Jerry just moved into their house and that he was really mean and that her wolf daddy was going to bite his throat and kill him at night.

She went on to tell me that the boyfriend hated it when she howled and said that her dad was dead and that she needed to get over it, and then he would hit her. She said she really hated him because he hurt her every day. I told her that I was going to get her some help because no one should ever hit her, especially with a belt. She hugged me and said her mom was going to be very mad that she told me. I told her that I was pretty sure her mom would want us to protect her.

Oh course, I immediately got our school counselor to help, and I called Child Protective Services. They came and talked to her and took pictures of the welts on her legs and bottom. Some of them had scabbed over, but her little bottom was a mess. The police arrested the boyfriend and things got very ugly for a while.

Amanda was put into foster care for about six weeks. She was so much happier and cleaner. She almost completely stopped howling and talking about her dad. She did her work and progressed amazingly quickly. She knew the whole alphabet and most of the sounds, and she could now count to 23.

They put her back with her mom right before Christmas. I was worried sick the whole Christmas break. When the kids came back to school in January, the old Amanda was back. She was howling again and talking about her dad. I asked her how her Christmas went. She told me that her mom's boyfriend got out of jail and that he and her mom had a huge fight and that her mom made him move out and that she never wanted to see him again but that she is going to because of the baby. I didn't even know the whole story, but I knew I wanted to cry.

Her mom picked her up from school that day and actually thanked me for turning her into social services. She said they had helped her a lot. She was taking parenting classes, and they got someone to help clean up her house and teach her how to cope with Amanda. She informed me that she was going to have the boyfriend's baby in June, which messed up her plans because she was going to move back to California with her mother. But now, her baby daddy was going to force her to stay in Idaho. She told me that she was going to be a better mother for this baby than she was for Amanda because she was 20 now and could handle it better. (She had Amanda when she was 14)

Towards the end of the school year, I started talking to her mom about possibly retaining Amanda in second grade. Her age was a year behind the rest of the students, and she was socially and emotionally a year behind the other students, too. I explained that she would go from being the farthest behind in class to being the farthest ahead, or at least closer to their level.

At first, her mother said "No way." Then I showed her Amanda's testing and her work and how far behind the other students she was. She started to notice the huge differences in her abilities to those of the other children. She finally agreed. I had to convince my principal, and then she had to convince the school district. It was quite the process, but I had enough evidence that they finally agreed.

We finally talked to Amanda about it. She didn't want her friends to move on without her. I told her that I needed her to be my special assistant to help me with the new first graders coming in. That seemed to appease her, and she finally agreed because I made sure she knew it was a special job.

The second year was so much better. She learned and grew so much. She was helping the other kids learn. She would help me explain the stories and some of the projects. It was such a good decision to hold her back. She told the kids that she was supposed to be in third grade but that Miss Melanie needed her to be her assistant, so she stayed to help them. It made her feel really special. The bonus fact was that her howling and communicating with her deceased father stopped. She acted like she didn't need him anymore.

Her mom had a baby sister in June. Amanda loved her so much. I think she thought she was the mother. She would tell me every day about how her sister was growing and spitting and was getting a tooth and crying and burping and pooping. She was so proud of her. She loved picking out her clothes and getting her dressed. I noticed that she was caring for and had a lot of responsibility for the baby.

Amanda was still struggling with reading. For some reason, she had given up on becoming a better reader. Towards the end of the second year, I noticed that her learning was slowing way down. She didn't seem to care very much anymore about school. I became very concerned and called her mom to ask for a parent-teacher conference. She told me that she didn't have time to come in and talk to me so we would have to talk over the phone.

She explained that they were fighting a lot with the baby's father because he wouldn't let them leave the state, and she really wanted to move back to California with her mom so that she could help her with the baby. She said that Amanda was the only one who could get the baby to calm down, so she would get her up at night to help with the baby. Poor little girl was exhausted. She said she didn't have time to help Amanda with her school work and that I would need to do that at school because she (the mom) needed to sleep when the baby did. I begged her to please read with her, but she said they didn't have time for that.

I was heartbroken when I would find Amanda asleep at her desk or on the floor in the reading center or under a table or in the lunchroom. I contacted social services again and explained how well she had been doing but how her learning had stopped. They tried to help, but the mom wasn't really willing to change anything.

Amanda became more and more withdrawn from me. She didn't want to talk to me anymore. I'm not sure what was actually happening, and I talked to her case workers, but they weren't sure either. She had had so much growth and had had such a great year until the end. It was hard to watch.

I passed her on to the third grade, knowing she still had deficits, but feeling unable to help her anymore. I was so disappointed. She started third grade, but her teacher told me that she didn't seem to have any will or interest in learning. Her mother pulled her out of school in the middle of third grade, saying she was going to homeschool her and needed her to help take care of the baby. I am still so worried about that little one. They moved shortly after her mom pulled her out of school, and I have tried to find out what happened to her since. I am guessing that the mom took the girls and left town so that the baby's father couldn't find them. I pray for Amanda and hope with all my heart that her wolf-daddy is actually somehow protecting her.

29

ANGELA

One of the hardest things ever for me to admit is when, as a teacher, I fail. After several years of teaching I finally learned that I could not save every child no matter how hard I tried. It's hard to say, but sometimes, I can't make up for bad parenting.

I had taught Angela's older brother, and I knew he had a tough life. He had two moms who had been in and out of jail with drug and shoplifting issues. They were very unstable and abusive. Her brother had been willing to let me into his life and into his heart. He knew that I cared about him and that I could break through his tough shell, and he started to care about learning and about himself because he knew that I cared about him. He had huge growth in second grade even though his home life was a disaster.

Angela, however, was a different story. She was one of the toughest, meanest girls I have ever met. She was a bully and said horrible things to the other kids. She was a loner and didn't care that nobody liked her. What she wanted, she got, or she would hit and kick and intimidate until she got what she wanted.

Angela confided in me one day and said, "Do you know what, Teacher? I am pretty sure that one of my moms is gay."

Trying not to laugh, I said, "That is very interesting."

She went on and said, "No, it's not interesting. It makes me mad, and I think I should kill them." I thought the first part of her statement was so funny that I started to giggle, but when she threatened to kill them, I was taken aback. I was shocked at the knowledge this child had about life and crime.

One day, Angela wanted to show us a trick that her moms had taught her. She had worn a dress so she could show us how one of her moms had taught her how to shoplift. I was fascinated by her explanation of layering clothes so the employees won't notice that you were stealing because you put your clothes back on top. She told us that the reason she wears dresses is to carry things out of the store between her knees. It actually took me a minute to realize that she was teaching us about actually shoplifting.

She told us she had been caught at K-Mart and that she now had a probation and parole officer (case worker) who checked up on her all the time. She acted like it was no big deal, but I made sure that the other children realized that it was a huge deal and very wrong and a crime and that they should never shoplift. I warned them that those kinds of choices would affect their whole future. Angela thought it was cool that she had a record and that the police knew who she was.

Another time for Show-and-Tell, she asked me if we could all go outside so she could show us something she had learned and that it would be a good activity for P.E. We all went outside, and she had us gather around the tetherball pole. She proceeded to show us how one of her mothers had taught her to dance. She was sliding up and down the pole and gyrating and hanging on to the pole. She knew some very sexy moves.

She also told us that you get more money if you flipped your hair. As soon as I realized what we were watching, I stopped it immediately and explained that it was inappropriate. I was shocked that a second grader even had this kind of knowledge. This was such odd and mature behavior for such a young girl that I was unprepared for what was happening. What second grader teaches pole dancing for Show-and-Tell? Once again, I assured the other kids that this is not what second graders needed to know and that it was something they didn't need to think or worry about ever.

From then on, Angela had to clear all her Show-and-Tells with me before she could share. I turned down crotchless panties, a black-lace bra, and a money clip that one of the men who visited their house had left, which she loved because it had a ruby on it and a roach holder for smoking weed. (I had to ask about this one because I had no idea what it was.) She would get very frustrated with me when I wouldn't let her share these items. I tried to explain that kids shouldn't even know about these things because they were grown-up things. She told me that that was a stupid rule.

To say that I was naïve around this child was a gigantic understatement. She had knowledge of things in the world that I didn't even know were things in the world. Her language was atrocious. I literally had to ask people if some of the things she called others were actually swear words and was informed that they were the worst things you can call people. I got a really inappropriate education from this child.

Her older brother had made sure she was in my class because he told me she was out of control and that he thought I was her only hope. I worked tirelessly with her. I would talk to her about choices and about the kind of person she wanted to be when she grew up. I explained that now was the time to choose if she wanted to go to jail or if she wanted to be a police officer and help other people who went to jail. She told me she had always wanted to be a police officer so she could bash people's heads in.

I spent hours researching how to teach children about empathy and about how to care about others. Honestly, nothing I tried worked with her. I was unable to get either of her mothers to come in and visit with me. I talked to one of them once, and she told me that dealing with Angela was my problem and that sort of stuff was what I got paid for and to never bother them again. Her exact words were, "You're the bitch that gets paid to deal with the little shit, and you need to earn your money and not put it back on us, so you better the hell deal with it and leave us alone."

I didn't really know what to say, so she hung up on me.

I sought help from everyone I could think of including the school counselor, the principal, social services, and her case worker. They all tried to help, but honestly, nothing really worked.

Academically, Angela was low. She didn't really seem to care about learning. As a teacher, in addition to building a child's I.Q. (intelligence quotient), I try to build their H.Q. (heart-quotient), too. After much prayer and contemplation, I decided that my time would best be spent trying to help her build some survival skills. I knew in order to survive the life she was choosing that she needed to know how to read. We focused a lot of time on her reading and math skills. I would often keep her in during recess to work with her. It had a twofold benefit. One, she learned how to read, and two, she didn't hurt the other kids.

Nearly every day, I would remind her that she could choose to be a criminal or a crime-fighter. Some days, she wanted to save the world, and other days, she wanted to kill her neighbors. I worked hard to try to understand how her brain worked, but I had to work harder to protect the other kids from her. She was a very frustrating little brown-eyed, brown-haired bully. She was physically a beautiful child, but she usually had a disgusted look on her face. I never saw her smile. I never heard her laugh.

After spring break, a little girl in our class named Gilly was showing us her new jacket she had received for her birthday. Gilly was a golden-blonde beauty with long flowing hair. She had huge blue eyes and was a tiny little child. Her parents were both professors at the local college. She was an only child and well cared for. She was a little spoiled, but she was a hard worker and had a quiet, delightful demeanor. She always wore beautiful clothes, and her hair was always picture perfect. Her new jacket was covered with sparkly rhinestones. It had a peace sign in silver rhinestones and a large rainbow in all the other colors of rhinestones. The kids *oohed* and *ahhed* at the jacket. The jacket was gray and matched her skirt. She was adorable with rainbow ribbons tied into her pigtails.

Gilly asked me if I liked her jacket. I told her it was amazing and that I was so happy that she had had a great birthday. Jokingly, I asked if I could borrow her jacket sometime and wear it because I had a gray skirt too. She giggled and said the sleeves were too short for my long arms. She was adorable.

I asked Gilly if she wanted to hang her jacket up on her hook, but she said she didn't want to because she didn't want to lose it. I agreed that it was a real treasure. She wore it all morning, and the kids commented on how it was gleaming and sparkly, and one little girl even called it radiant. (Good vocabulary practice, I thought.)

I had noticed Angela watching the whole interaction, but she had stayed very quiet, so I assumed she wasn't interested in the jacket at all. I have never been so wrong in my life.

As I was bringing the kids in from lunch recess, one of our parapros named Louise came in with the kids. She said that she would be taking over my classroom because the principal needed me in his office. I was surprised and quickly prepared Louise to take over.

As I walked down the hall, I noticed two police officers standing outside of the principal's office. There were about five or six fifth graders there, also, and the police were talking to them. The secretary was in the sick room with Gilly. She was putting bandages on her, and Gilly was holding a bag of ice on her face. I went to Gilly and gathered her in my arms. She was sobbing. I started rocking her and trying to figure out what had happened. The secretary told me that it was really bad and Gilly's parents were on their way to the school to take her to the hospital.

A few minutes later, Gilly's parents walked in, and her mom took her from me. They, like me, didn't know what had happened either. The principal came out and asked them to take her to the hospital and call as soon as they could identify her injuries. The whole scene was awful. Gilly's dad carried her to the car. I was still unsure what had happened. I just knew that Gilly seemed hurt bad.

The principal asked me to come into his office. There sat Angela with a female police officer. The principal informed me that her case worker was on her way. The principal looked at Angela, who was gripping tightly to the handles of the chair. She seemed very angry. He said to her, "Would you like to tell your teacher what happened, or should I?"

Angela screamed, "I just wanted the G**damned jacket. What the hell is the big f***ing deal?" I covered my mouth, shocked, as I had not heard that kind of language come out of a child so young in my life.

Staying very calm, the principal turned to me and explained that Angela had asked some of her brother's fifth grade friends to help her get the jacket away from Gilly. Incredibly frustrated, he said, "And for some unknown reason, they agreed. So, apparently, Angela asked Gilly if she would come with her to the top of the hill to show the fifth graders her jacket." He turned to Angela and said, "Please tell your teacher why you took her to the top of the hill."

There was a long pause. She finally blurted, "There aren't any f****ing cameras up there, okay? What the hell is the big deal?"

Our school has cameras all around the outside and inside of the school, but they do not reach the top of the hill, and you can't see what is happening because it's too far away. I do not know how Angela knew that and was amazed that she figured that out before she committed her crime.

The principal went on. "Angela demanded that Gilly give her the jacket. Gilly said 'No' and tried to walk away. Angela grabbed her hair and threw her to the ground. Then she yelled at her to give her the jacket right now. Once again, Gilly said, 'No, please let me go,' to which Angela responded by kicking her and told the other girls to kick her, too. So, they all proceeded to kick her until Angela was able to rip the jacket off of her. Other kids saw them surrounding Gilly and ran to get the para-pro on duty. They stopped the attack immediately, but by then, they had torn the jacket off of Gilly, and Angela had it hidden under her shirt. Gilly was badly injured!"

My eyes filled with tears as I looked at Angela, who was smiling. She showed no remorse. I seriously think she thought it was funny. The jacket was lying on the principal's desk. The sleeve was torn, and some of the rhinestones were gone. The principal just sat there and shook his head. We were both shocked. The police officer said that they were going to charge her with assault and battery. They had tried to get ahold of her mother, but her phone had been turned off. The officers asked me if I had anything to say. I honestly didn't know what to say. Tears rolled down my cheeks as I looked at this beautiful 7-year-old child, who thought what she had just done was funny. She just kept saying, "I wanted the f***ing jacket. I can't believe you guys are making such a big-ass deal about it!"

The whole situation seriously hurt my heart. I thought I was having a heart attack. I felt like I had been run over by a truck. The police officers interviewed all of the other girls involved. They were all suspended for two days. There were some shocked parents who were amazed that their daughters were involved in beating up a tiny second grader. Some of the girls said they did it because they were afraid that Angela's brother would beat them up if they didn't, and some said they were afraid of Angela. She lived in their neighborhood and they had seen the awful things she did to people's property and their pets.

The police officers took Angela home. Her mother had a "shit-fit," as Angela told me later, but her mothers were mad at me because I let it happen. They felt that I should have been watching Angela to make sure she didn't beat anyone up. They felt that I should be fired and that the school district should take action against me. They told the police officers that they sent her to school so that I could keep her out of trouble and that if I couldn't do that then I needed to be fired. They said they were going to file a formal complaint against me. They refused to pay for a new jacket for Gilly (I bought her a new jacket) and said that they couldn't help it if some spoiled little rich girl got her feelings hurt. She didn't need a jacket anyway and it served her right for flaunting it at school and what did she expect to happen, the little whore. Apparently, the police officers stopped them then and refused to listen to anything else they had to say.

The police officers explained what had happened to the principal, who then told me. He said that the police officers were willing to back me up if they really did go through with trying to get me fired. The principal had already contacted the Director of Elementary Education, and she was going to stand behind me all the way, as she knew that I had tried very hard to help this little girl. I was truly filled with a deep, dark sadness, and I was shaking. I felt I had failed both little girls.

Angela was suspended from school for a week. Gilly was physically all right, but she had cuts and bruises and a black eye because Angela had kicked her in the face. Emotionally, however, she was a mess. Her parents got her into some counseling. They were great and very caring. They had threatened to take her to a different school, but they were impressed how the kids in my class rallied around her and begged her not to leave. They knew how much I tried to protect her and how much I loved and cared about her. I had been working with them all year, and they knew it wasn't my fault. From then on, I made sure that Angela and Gilly were never together.

Angela went on like nothing had even happened. Gilly stayed very close to me whenever Angela was around. The other girls all got citations in their school records, but if they didn't get into any more trouble, their records would be expunged. Angela's record would not be expunged, however. Her crime would remain on her permanent record because the juvenile judge felt people should know how devious she was.

When Angela came back to school from her suspension, I had an idea that I hoped would help. The principal was able to get permission from her mothers, and I had arranged with our school social worker to have Angela spend a day at the juvenile justice facility. I was hoping that it would scare her into making better choices. I explained that she had to do everything they said and that she had no freedom to do what she wanted. She had to do everything they told her, and in the juvenile justice facility, she had no choices. I was trying to scare her straight. I told her that prison is not a nice place and that she would really hate it there.

Man, oh man, did that ever go wrong. When she returned to school after a day at juvy, she went on and on about how clean it was there. She told the kids that she would get her own bed and not have to sleep on the couch or the floor and that she got to eat real food and that it was so bright there and they didn't even yell at her. Wowzers! Did that ever backfire. For the rest of the year, she would tell us that she couldn't wait to get to juvy. I tried like crazy to get her to want to be on the police-officer side of crime, but she was too excited about the clean place, her own bed, and food every day.

I knew I had failed this little person. I have wondered many times since then what happened to her. I do know that her criminal case worker dealt with her many times after she left my class. I wish with all of my heart that I could have made a difference in her little life and in her future.

30

ISAAC

Another one of the hardest things for me to admit as a teacher is that there are a few kids, very few, that I just don't like. I know it's awful to say. Early in my career, I must admit that I didn't work as hard as I do now to get to know and appreciate each little one put in my care.

One of the best pieces of advice I received as a teacher came from the self-talk I had at the end of the day. Now, every day, when I get in my car to go home, I say a little prayer that goes something like this: "Heavenly Father, thank you for my amazing job and my wonderful children. Especially thank you for Brenna, Adria, Tayzley, Camden, Anthem, Griffin, Hazel, Drayson, Molly, Anna, Max, Alexis, Ausie, etc. (I list all the kids who are great little kids and are not behaviorally challenged.) Now Heavenly Father, can we talk about Isaac. (I have found that if you only focus on the kids you want to complain about, your job seems very daunting and a lot harder.)"

If you only have two kids out of 25 who are giving you concern, you have a pretty great job, and nothing seems so hard anymore. If you focus all your attention on the two or three kids that are giving you fits, you'll suffer a lot. It's a difficult thing to do because, often, the two or three trouble-makers are all consuming.

Shortly after I transferred to second grade, I had a boy in my class named Isaac. He was a large Hispanic boy and was at least a head taller than all of the other children. (I found out later that he was a year older than the other children.) He had black, curly hair, dark eyes, and a scowl on his face. He already had his permanent teeth. He acted and talked like a bully. He would tell the other kids that he was going to "put the hurt" on them.

It was evident that all of the kids in my class were afraid of him. One of his favorite activities was to take the red classroom ball outside to recess. He would bounce it around for a while and then throw it as hard as he could to see if he could knock one of the kids down. He would tell me that he just wanted someone to play with him. I tried to explain that people don't want to play with people who hurt them. He just snarled at me and said, "Man, we have a bunch of big babies in this class. They should all be crying boo-hoo, boo-hoo."

I stopped letting him take the ball out.

Over the years, I have found that most of the kids I have worked with who are bullies have learned to be bullies at home or somewhere else in their lives. This is why it's so important that we minimize exposure to bullying and provide environments that prevent it, all while cultivating more positive forms of social interaction.

Isaac was a very angry child. I didn't take the time to figure out why. He would argue with me about everything. He was very disrespectful and crass. He loved to pick on kids that were littler than him, which, by-the-way, was everyone. All day long, I would ask him to change his behavior. He would stomp off and complain under his breath so I couldn't understand him.

His bullying got worse and worse. Instead of talking to him and trying to understand him, I just contacted the principal and asked for help. They would talk, and it would be better for a while, but he would always go back to his previous behavior.

One day, we were having a particularly bad day. He was being very destructive. He was breaking pencils and scissors on purpose, tearing things off the wall, and knocking stuff off other kids' desks. He loved to walk by and kick over the garbage cans so garbage would spill out onto the floor. I would ask him to pick it up. He would argue with me, then one of the other kids would pick it up and clean up the garbage to get him to stop arguing. It was definitely a power struggle, and I was losing.

Isaac was working at the computer station on this particular day. His computer was very slow, so he got impatient and started pounding on the keys of the computer. I asked him to stop, as he would damage the computer. He looked at me and hit it harder. I said, "Isaac, please don't hit the computers. They are having a hard enough time already." He stuck out his tongue at me and slapped the keyboard as hard as he could.

I walked up behind him and grabbed his wrists to keep him from hitting the keyboard again.

To say he flipped out was an understatement. He went crazy. He jumped up from the computer and screamed at me, "Don't you ever touch me — I mean ever — or I will kill you!"

Everyone in the classroom froze. Isaac started pacing back and forth and ranting, "Nobody better touch me, nobody better touch me, nobody better touch me!" over and over again. He was getting madder and madder.

He started to walk around the room in a big circle. He was muttering and freaking out. He was stomping and pulling his hair and hitting his head with his fists. As he walked back by the coat rack, he started throwing backpacks onto the ground. Then he started circling the kids again. One of the little girls ran back to grab her backpack to hang it back up. When Isaac saw her, he circled around and stomped on her hand. I knew we were in danger, and I had to protect the other children.

I tried to stay calm. I said to the children, "We need to do a room clear. Will you carefully and quietly walk into the library for a few minutes until we can calm things down?"

Isaac screamed, "No, they are going to stay here!"

I took a deep breath and said, "Isaac, you are very upset now, but I can't let you hurt the other kids, so I am going to have them go to a safe place."

He started screaming at me and picked up a chair and threw it at me. He turned into a wild creature.

As quickly as possible, I shuffled all the children out of the room. Some of them wanted to grab their backpacks and coats, but I explained that they just needed to leave as quickly as possible. They were scared to death and did what I asked them to do. As they got to the library, the librarian came to my room to see what was happening and called for help. Isaac was throwing chairs and knocking over tables and being as destructive as possible.

The principal was out of the building at the time, so the secretary and the librarian came in to try to help me. They wanted to surround him and try to stop him from causing so much damage. I said I didn't think we should touch him and that I thought we needed to call the police. Isaac roared, "You better not call the police!" I was working my way toward the door, trying not to get hit by flying chairs.

The secretary left the room to call the police, and the librarian left the room to go help my other students. I said to Isaac, "Okay buddy, let's see if we can calm down a little!" He went crazy and dumped out a desk and picked it up and chucked it at me. I knew I was making things worse.

I went out of the classroom, closed the door, and watched through the window. At first, he charged the door trying to get out, but I had it blocked because I could tell he wanted to hurt someone.

For the next 15 minutes, while we waited for the police, Isaac built an impressive fortress in my room that blocked the door. He piled desks and chairs in front of the door so that no one could get in. He dumped out the desks and threw piles of papers onto the floor. He dumped out the garbage cans and was making as big a mess as he possibly could. I have never seen anyone so out of control.

In addition to calling the police, our secretary called Isaac's mom. Her first question was "What did the teacher do to him? She hates him, and he knows it." Later, when the secretary told me that, I felt terrible. I knew his mother was right. I had shown no kindness toward this kid. I was ashamed of myself and vowed I would never put another child in that position.

When the police arrived, I was outside the door watching through the window making sure that Isaac didn't hurt himself. At one point, I opened the door and asked him to please not ruin my guitar. He had some scissors and was going to cut the strings. He walked away and started cutting up paper instead. I opened the door again and thanked him for not ruining my guitar. He had dragged all the desks and tables over to the door to barricade himself inside. The barricade now blocked the whole doorway.

I explained to the officer what had happened. I told him that I had grabbed his wrists to get him to stop pounding on the computer and that had set him off and that he had been out of control ever since. I recounted how he had stomped on another child's hand and how I had done a room clear trying to protect them and that I thought that made him even madder. I admitted that I had done everything wrong in handling the situation. The officer explained that he felt I had handled it the best I could and that they would take it from there.

Just then, Isaac's mom came screaming down the hall. She came right up to me and screamed, "What the hell did you do to my son!?" That really shook me up. The other officer asked her to go with him, and they walked down to the principal's office to try to calm her down.

The first officer said to me, "Take some deep breaths and try to calm down. Please go and help your other children, as they are probably very upset, and we'll take care of this situation."

I was shaking, but I walked down the hall to the lunchroom. All the kids ran up to me to make sure I was okay. I was close to tears, and they could tell. They hugged me and said they were glad I was okay. We went outside and sat in a big circle, and everyone got a chance to talk about what had happened and how they felt about it.

I was amazed at how much concern they had for Isaac and his well-being. I told them how proud I was of them that they had done such a good job on the room clear and that they had been so calm in the library. I told them that we had a big mess we needed to clean up when we got back to class. I explained that I was going to need some Cinderella girls and some Cinderella boys to help me clean up our room. They thought that was hilarious.

The police took Isaac and his mom to the police station. We went back into our room and put on some Disney music and cleaned everything up. I gave each of the kids a piece of paper and asked them to write about what had happened and how they felt about it. I encouraged them to also include a drawing of what happened, too. The drawings turned out amazingly well. It was easy to tell how scared the kids were by the pictures they drew. Several of the kids drew pictures of Isaac bullying them. They all drew him with a mean, disgusted face. It was frightening.

Without mentioning Isaac specifically by name, I sent a note home to parents explaining what happened and that their child had done a great job of staying calm. I asked them to please talk to their child about their experience and how important it was that they feel safe at school. Most of the parents wrote notes back thanking me for helping their child stay safe. I don't think they had any idea how completely rattled I was. The kids and I did a Sharing Circle that next day and discussed what we did right and what we could have done better. We learned and grew a lot that day.

Apparently, Isaac and his family returned to Mexico the next week. The police explained that the mom went completely out of control at the police station and started hitting Isaac. They had to restrain her. She was yelling that he had ruined everything for their family. We never saw Isaac again.

I learned a lot from my experience with Isaac and his family. I now understand that all kids need to be cared about no matter how much they fight or how much they reject you. I must figure out a way to break through that hard shell of anger and find the kid that just wants to be loved. I wish I had handled the situation with Isaac better. I wish I had been kinder, and I wish I would have taken time to figure out how he felt and how he processed information. I wish I had learned to care about him and let him know that I did care.

31

RAMONA

There is a book from my childhood that I loved. It was about a little girl who was a scrappy little rag-a-muffin. She was a character I loved because she was very naughty and clever and funny. She drove her family and her teachers crazy and it warmed my heart. I remember spending many nights reading the books about her and always felt sad when the book ended. I remember wishing that she was my best friend. Her name was Ramona the Pest.

One year, much to my surprise, I had Ramona in my classroom. I am assuming that her mother loved the *Ramona the Pest* books, too. My Ramona was just as scrappy and adorable as the character in the beloved books. The first day I met her was a warm memory I'll never forget.

Her mom walked in the door and shook my hand and introduced herself. She turned to introduce Ramona, but she was nowhere to be found. Frustrated, her mom said, "I'm sorry. I'll go find her. She was right behind me." I followed her down the hall. Because this was the "Meet the Teacher Day" before school actually started, there weren't very many people in the school.

We heard noises coming from the library. I was surprised because the library was not open yet, and I couldn't figure out why someone would be in there. Our library is in the heart of our school, with halls and classrooms on two sides.

The library itself is a large open space. The half walls are created by bookcases. It has a little stage with large steps that the kids sit on so the librarian can read to them. Our librarian has collected many amazing things over the years for the kids to sit in and read. We have a train that holds eight kids, a ship that holds three kids, a barn that holds four kids, several couches and stools, and fancy chairs for the kids to enjoy while they read. One of everyone's favorite places in the library is the old-fashioned bathtub. The librarian found an antique white, clawed, stand-alone bathtub. She put two big, blue bean bag pillows in it. The kids love to lie on the bean bags and read books.

When Ramona's mom and I walked into the library, we found her. She had grabbed piles of books and was sitting in the bathtub looking at them. I knew the librarian would be upset because she would have to put all of the books back, but it was a really funny sight. She looked up at us and said, "I decided that I want school to start today!" I could tell that her mom was really embarrassed and apologized over and over again. She was trying to put the books back, but I told her she probably better let the librarian do that because she had a system.

Ramona got out of the bathtub and ran back to my room and immediately started exploring. She was pulling things out of drawers and off shelves. We quickly followed her, but she had already made a mess. She was speedy and destructive.

Her mother was embarrassed and started to clean up after her. I said, "How about letting Ramona clean up after herself?" They both looked at me like I was out of my mind. I went on. "Ramona, it's very nice to meet you, and I am excited that you're going to be in my class, but my rule is, if you get it out, it's your job to put it away."

Her mother said, "Good luck with that. I don't have the energy to make her clean up after herself. I had her when I was 47 years old, and she wears me out." The mom went on to tell me that Ramona was born with heart problems and has had seven open-heart surgeries since. She said it didn't seem to affect her energy more than it did for just a couple of days after the surgeries.

I went to Ramona and knelt. I asked her to look me in the eyes. I asked, "Ramona, do you like playing with the toys in here?" She nodded. I continued, "That is wonderful, but second graders clean up after themselves, so you can play with anything in the room while I visit with your mom, but if you choose to leave a mess, you're choosing to never play with them again. Do you understand? I need to know that you're ready for second grade."

She looked at her mother then back at me. Then, hesitantly, she nodded again. I said, "Sounds like we have a full-fledged second grader right here in our classroom."

Over the next 10 minutes, I explained the curriculum and what would be expected and found out how she was getting home from school. When it was time to go, I said to Ramona, "Guess what — it's time to go, so let's see if you can clean up everything you got out in two minutes. Do you think you can do it?"

She said, "I only need one!" She went crazy picking stuff up and putting it all away.

I said, "Hey, you started before I even said 'Ready, set, go!'" Her mom was in shock. She just stood there with her mouth open. Ramona was cleaning like a wild tornado.

When she was almost finished, I started to count down from 10. She finished, and she was sweating and smiling. I could tell she was proud of herself, and I gave her a high five. Her mom hugged me and thanked me and said she was thrilled to see what I could get her to do this year.

Ramona was a bit of a challenge, to say the least. She would have full-blown, stomp-her-feet-and-scream temper tantrums when she didn't get her way. She came to school with her beautiful long hair pulled back in a ponytail, and by lunchtime, it was loose and flying in the wind. She was a tiny ball of fire and felt that the whole world was against her.

During her temper tantrums, I would force myself not to react. She would look at me and wait for a response. I would watch the clock and time her tantrums. When she finally calmed down, I would say, "Hey, sweetie, that tantrum thing doesn't really work for me, so I need you to make up the time you wasted during recess. By the way, nice red face, and you win for the loudest scream I have ever heard." She would just stare at me, breathing and sweating. She would stomp to her desk, fold her arms, and pout. I would add that time to her recess break.

As the year went on, her temper tantrums got fewer and were over more quickly. By November, she didn't even have them anymore. I congratulated her and told her how proud I was of her and how impressed that she actually acted like a nearly perfect, little second grader. Even the other kids thanked her for not hurting their learning anymore. Every once in a while, she would still get really frustrated and have a mini temper tantrum, but it was nothing like it was at the beginning of the year.

Ramona was a yeller. Even when she talked, she yelled. I would ask her to please not yell at me. I could tell she didn't mean to. She wasn't mad; she just wanted to be heard. During parent-teacher conferences, both of Ramona's parents came to visit with me. I finally understood the yelling. Her mother had had her when she was 47, but her father had been 55 at the time. He was now 62 and refused to wear a hearing aide. Everyone compensated by yelling so he could hear them. Ramona hadn't figured out that she only needed to yell at him to be heard. We worked on solving the yelling problem all year.

Ramona was a lightbulb kid. You could watch the lightbulb come on in her head when she understood a new concept. Every day, I watched her figure something out, then she would yell excitedly, "OHHHHH, I GET IT!" and run and tell me what she had learned. I would ask her to tell me again without yelling at me. She would, but then she would jump up and down, so excited to tell me that she was about ready to explode because she couldn't yell. I love light-bulb kids. They are why I love teaching.

One morning, close to recess time, Ramona came up to me and asked if she could use the telephone pass to call her mother. I asked her if I could help her with something. She whispered in my ear that she had had an accident in her pants and needed some new clothes. I put my finger to my lips so that I wouldn't embarrass her. Her mom brought her some clean clothes.

Right before lunch, she came up to me again and signaled for me to bend over so she could whisper in my ear. She said she'd had another accident and could she please go call her mother again. I winked at her and handed her the phone pass, making sure the other kids didn't notice.

As I was bringing the kids in from recess, she pulled me aside, and this time, she didn't even have to say anything. She just pointed to the drawer where the phone pass was. I said, "Are you okay?" She shrugged her shoulders and skipped to the office to call her mom. I was feeling kind of bad for her by now.

We went on with the day. I was reading *Junie B. Jones* (love her too; she is a little bit naughty) to the kids. Ramona stood up and yelled, "Teacher, I need the phone pass right now!"

It took me by surprise, and I questioned, "Again?"

She was so serious, then she yelled as loud as she could. "Yes, Teacher, because every single time I fart, I poop my pants! Geez!" I sat there, speechless. I didn't know what to do or what to say — neither did the other kids.

Every one of us was staring at her, unsure of what to do next. I thought she was mad or embarrassed or having a temper tantrum or something, but she started to laugh and laugh. Thank goodness she thought it was hilarious. That gave us permission to laugh with her. The other kids started laughing and saying that they hated it when that happened to them, too. They hated it when they accidently pooped their pants. It ended up being super funny and a real bonding moment.

Ramona took the phone pass and called her mom again. This

time, her mom took her home and treated her for diarrhea. I was so impressed: no temper tantrum, no screaming, no stomping, just laughing. Wowzers. She came a long, long way that year. She'd love to yell at you about it!

32

VICTORIA

September 11, 2001, was a day that Americans will never forget. Most people remember every detail of that horrible day. My mom called me at 6:50 a.m. and said, "Turn on the T.V. Something terrible is happening!" I was brushing my teeth and preparing to go to school. In Idaho, it was 6:45 when the first plane hit the north tower of the World Trade Center in New York City. I watched with horror as the worst day in American history started to unfold.

By the time I got to school at 7:50, I had heard that another plane had hit the south tower. As soon as I walked into my classroom, I turned on the T.V. to see what was happening. The only thing on the T.V. was static. It was obvious that we were not getting the satellite feed. I walked to the office to ask the principal what was happening. The secretary told me that the principal was gone to meetings, but that she had told her to turn off the internet feed to the building. Not only could we not get the news, we couldn't go on any of the other websites designed to help us fulfill our educational goals. It was a black-out!

Luckily, we could keep our cell phones with us and keep them on. My husband called me right before we brought the kids in and told me that a plane had hit the Pentagon. Everyone was in shock, but we couldn't get any information about what was happening. The next text I got from my husband said that President Bush had come on the T.V. and announced that America was at war. It was surreal because everything in Idaho seemed so normal.

As I brought my students in, almost every one of them told me about the planes hitting the buildings. They didn't know where New York City was and wanted to know if a plane was going to crash into our school. I tried to calm them down by showing them where New York City is compared to where Idaho is. I explained that it's a long way away and that we felt sad for the people in the planes and in the buildings.

We tried to go on like it was a normal day. Our principal had blacked out all the information happening, but we knew enough to make it very uncomfortable and tense. My husband texted to tell me that one of the World Trade Center buildings had collapsed and that thousands of people were dead. I didn't tell the kids, but I'm sure they could feel that something was amiss, as I was very shaken.

Victoria came into the classroom about ten minutes after the tardy bell rang. I could tell she was upset. She came right over to me, hugged me, and started to cry. I sat down and gathered her in my arms. As I stroked her hair, she started to tell me that she had seen some planes run into some big buildings and that a whole bunch of people died. She said, "My heart breaked." I tried to calm her down, but she was scared and so sad. I held her for a while.

She finally said, "What about my grandma? What if she gets hit by the plane?" I wasn't real sure what to say, as I didn't know the situation and thought maybe her grandma lived in New York City.

I finally asked her where her grandma lives. She looked at me and said, "In a really tall city." She said she didn't know which city she lived in, but she knew she lived in a huge, tall apartment that touched the sky. She laid her head on my shoulder and sobbed again. I couldn't seem to help her at all, and she was making the other kids upset. I decided to let her go and call her mom and ask her if her grandma was okay. Our secretary helped her make the phone call. Her mother said her grandma was fine.

When Victoria came back to the classroom, she tried hard to participate in the activity we were doing. I could tell she was still worried and on the verge of tears. At recess, she came and asked if she could sit on my lap again. She told me that her grandma was lovely and that she loved her so much because she got to sleep at her house sometimes and look down. She told me that the people were little and the cars were tiny, too, and it was really fun to watch all of the mini-people. I was trying so hard to comfort her, but I wasn't sure what to say. She started to cry again.

When the other kids came in, Victoria ate snacks with them and said the Pledge of Allegiance. We tried to work on math, but nobody seemed to be able to concentrate. I finally came up with a math game that interested the kids enough to play and keep them occupied. Victoria was still upset, but she did her best to participate.

After I walked the kids to lunch, I talked to my husband, and he informed me that both World Trade Center buildings had fallen and that another plane had crashed into a field in Pennsylvania. He said people were jumping out of the towers to their deaths before the buildings fell. He said the world was watching and that people were horrified.

The whole world was watching — except for the people at our school.

During the lunch break, I called Victoria's mom and explained that she was having a real tough time. I told her that she was really worried about her grandma. I asked her if there was any way her grandma could call and talk to her and let Victoria know she was okay. She said she would try.

When the kids came in from lunch recess, I read to them. Victoria leaned against my leg and started to cry again. I rubbed her head, unsure what else to do to help. She lay down on the floor and sobbed. I rubbed her back.

Later on that afternoon, our secretary called into my room and asked if Victoria could come to the phone and talk to her grandma. She jumped up and literally ran down the hall.

When she came back to our room, she was beaming. She ran to

me and squealed, "My grandma is alive, and the planes didn't crash into her big building and kill her dead, and she called me Little Vicky because that's what she calls me, and she said I could come to her house and watch all of the mini people with her again." She hugged me repeatedly. She was so happy and joyful.

I thought I better try and figure out what she was thinking and why she was so traumatized. She explained to me that her grandma lived in Salt Lake City in a really, really tall building. When she saw the planes on T.V. hit the buildings in New York City, she thought they were in Salt Lake City and had hit her grandma's building. She told me that she thought planes hit all the big buildings in all of the cities in the world, and so she thought her grandma got burned up.

"Oh, my goodness," I said. "That must have been so terribly frightening for you." I hugged her again.

The tragedies of September 11, 2001, were horrible and life changing. We were sheltered from the events of that day as they unfolded, but were devastated by the aftermath. When the kids got home from school, they saw the planes hit the buildings over and over again on television. Their parents explained to them what had happened. They were glad I had showed them where New York City was, and they knew that Idaho was super far away. It helped them feel safer, but they knew that America had changed.

The next day, we had a Sharing Circle, and all the kids explained how they felt about what had happened and talked about the things their parents had told them. We made an American flag out of paper, and we did tear art on it. We say the Pledge of Allegiance every day and have great respect for the flag. The kids tore red, white, and blue paper into little pieces and then glued them onto a pencil draft of a flag. I explained that most people in America felt like they had been torn apart by the events that had happened the day before. The flags looked like they had been torn apart and then mended back together. One of the kids said that it looked like America did on September 11. "We gotted torn apart, but now we are getting glued back together." They were awesome, but they looked very sad.

The kids wrote about what happened and how they felt about it. They drew pictures of the towers and the planes crashing into them. I was amazed at how accurate the drawings were and then realized that the kids had seen the news footage repeatedly at home.

Most of the pictures the kids drew were eerily similar. Except one. Victoria drew a beautiful picture with tiny World Trade Center towers in the background with tiny planes hitting them. In the front of the drawing, she drew a picture of her grandma hugging her and smiling with hearts all around them. It was precious and tragic and heartwarming.

33

MADDOX

Halloween is one of my favorite holidays during the school year. We have found that most children, especially children of poverty, adore Halloween. I'm not sure if it's because they love to escape their real lives for an evening or if they love getting free candy or if the costumes are intriguing or if it's because their parents seem to love Halloween, too.

We have tons of parent's volunteer on Halloween. They love to see their children dressed up, and they love to help with parties. Some schools have gotten away from celebrating Halloween, but at our school, it's a highlight of the year.

Unfortunately, we have had to set some strict rules for the students and their costumes and even for the parents. I have been amazed at how many times I have had to tell little girls that they can't come to school dressed as a dead hooker, a serial singer who kills people, or a stripper (boys and girls).

Over the years, I've been pretty shocked by some of the costumes that my little second graders wore on Halloween. One little boy came dressed as a giant sperm, and another little boy came as a Chip and Dale dancer complete with a thong, a G-string, and bare chest with hair drawn on. On year, one of my students came dressed as the Columbine high school shooter complete with a trench coat and toy rifle.

But the worst costume I ever saw was a little second grade girl who came dressed like an abortion. She had bloodied baby doll parts pinned all over her and red paint to look like blood smeared everywhere. For the life of me, I couldn't understand what parents were thinking. When I had the children call home and say their costumes were inappropriate for school, occasionally, the parents were surprised. Clearly, we as teachers and parents need to communicate, so we have since shared expectations.

Most parents send their adorable little princesses and knights and monsters and ghosts and ninjas to school. The kids get to do a school-wide parade so they can see all the costumes. The parents form a line on the playground and watch and cheer for their little ones as they pass by and wave. Then the kids go back to their room for a class party. In my class, we have a fashion show, so the kids can show off their adorable costumes.

The other thing that makes me laugh about Halloween is how many parents dress themselves up in costumes to join their children at school. We have seen some fun and interesting (and inappropriate) costumes on parents. The parents' costumes are often hilarious, but not really appropriate for an elementary school setting. It's a little bit funny when the principal must ask them to go home and change because their costume is not appropriate for children to see. I laugh a little bit. Okay, I laugh a lot when he gets to tell them that.

One year, we had a great party. I had seven parents show up to help with the games. Four of them were wearing costumes, and I assigned the parents to different stations to run the activities. We had a Monster Math station, a spelling scramble station, a build-a-story obstacle course, a penny-toss addition station, a create-a-creature station, and a monster toast-making station. The kids traveled around the room to the different games. It was a blast.

Maddox was a dark-haired, adorable brown-eyed munchkin. He had lost his front teeth and was unable to say his Rs or his Ls.

During the party, he came up to me and put his hands on his hips and said, "Teachew, we have a pwobwem."

I smiled at him and said, "Please tell me about our problem!"

He whispered to me, "Weww (well), you know the wady who is hewping us make Monstew Toast?"

I said, "Yes, she is wonderful, isn't she?"

He said, "Weww, hew bwestacle felled out of her shiwt, and evewyone can see it."

I giggled because he said it so funny and so fast that I didn't understand anything he had just said. I didn't have any idea what he was talking about.

He took a deep breath and said it again. "Dat wady's bwesticle came out of hew shiwt." He was very excited and was talking really fast, but I still was not understanding, so he started yelling at me and said, cupping his hands out in front of his chest, "You know, my dad caws them bwesticles, but my mom caws them boobies, and my bwothew caws them tits. And that wady's fell out of her shiwt."

I finally got it and was laughing so hard. I walked over to the adorable mother who was dressed as Cleopatra and was working hard helping the kids. Indeed, one of her breasts was definitely exposed. I motioned for her to cover up. She was completely unaware of it and was super embarrassed. Not only did she cover up, but she put on her sweater as well. I felt so bad for her, but I smiled and waved like it was no big deal.

Maddox returned to finishing his monster toast and said, "Thank you, Teacher. By the way, supew fun pawty." He went right back to painting his bread like nothing had happened. The poor mother was horrified and kept looking at me apologetically, but I gave her a thumbs up as if it hadn't even happened. It seemed that nobody else had noticed anyway.

After the kids left for the day, the mother was helping me clean up and kept apologizing over and over again. I explained to her what had happened and how I found out and that I could not understand what Maddox was trying to tell me. I had no idea what a "bwestacle" was. I am sure his dad hadn't intended for us to ever find out either. We laughed and laughed about the mishap.

A few days later, I talked to Maddox's dad. His dad asked me what had happened, as he couldn't understand what Maddox was trying to tell him. He was super embarrassed when I explained that I couldn't understand what he was telling me and that he was using a word I didn't know. I made sure not to let him know who the mother was, but told him we had had a great laugh. He said he hadn't even realized that Maddox had heard him and that Maddox, not being able to pronounce his Rs, would get him into so much trouble. He apologized for making up the word breasticles and said he would go home and wash his mouth out with soap. I reminded him that kids hear and repeat everything. We had a good laugh about the whole thing.

34

MARCUS, JR

Marcus Jr. was a beautiful black child. He was tall and strong and thin. He was a very handsome young man. His father was from Zimbabwe, and his mother was from Detroit. They had met at a college in Chicago. They had recently moved to Pocatello so both parents could finish their master's degrees at our local university. Marcus Sr. was about 6'7", and his wife, Asia, was 6'1". They were both basketball players.

I met the whole family at Meet-the-Teacher Night. Marcus and his dad called each other Junior or Senior respectively.

Asia, the mom, followed suit. I asked if he wanted us to call him Marcus or Junior. He looked at his mom, and she said, "It's up to you, buddy."

Marcus asked, "Can I think about it for a bit?" I told him, as I did when I welcomed all of the kids, that I was super excited to be his teacher and that he could tell me his decision about his name on the first day of school. They also had a beautiful 1-year-old daughter. They were a remarkable family. I was super impressed with all of them.

On the first day of school, Marcus, Jr. told me that he wanted to be called Junior, so I introduced him that way. As the rest of the kids came in, he watched everyone very carefully. As we were all gathering around, he whispered to me, "Teacher, where are all the Afro-American people?"

I said, "Well, Junior, you are it! Isn't that awesome? You're super special because you are different and so handsome. You have amazing eyes and a fantastic smile. You are so lucky!" He smiled at me and said, "Okay, I guess I'll be the only Afro-American dude!" It was so cute.

Junior was very bright and loved to learn. He got along with everyone and became fast friends, especially with all the boys. He was funny and joyful. The kids asked him questions about his skin and his hair and why his teeth were so white. He explained that his dad was from Africa and his mom was from Detroit and there are a lot of African-American people there. One of the little girls asked him if she could touch his arm to see if the black would rub off. I held my breath, praying she hadn't offended him. He said, "Can I touch your arm and see if the tan rubs off?" Then he started to laugh and then everyone laughed. I breathed a huge sigh of relief.

I explained to Junior that there was a lot of curiosity about him, and I told him how much I appreciated how patient and kind he was to everyone. I told him that I wished we had more Afro-American, Hispanic, and Native American people in our town and especially in our school. I thanked him for helping me teach the kids about different races and told my students that they were so lucky to have him as a friend. Most of the kids in my class said they had never seen an African-American person before and were thrilled to have a friend who was so open about sharing experiences that they had not been aware of. He asked me once if the kids thought they were all the same color because they were white.

I replied, "Wow, that is a really interesting question. I honestly don't know the answer. Maybe you could ask them."

He said, "Okay, I will!" He came back a few minutes later and told me that one of the boys had told him that girls are "pinker" than boys. I literally laughed out loud. So did Junior!

One morning, Junior came in from the playground, and he

wasn't wearing a coat. He was shivering. There were two feet of snow on the ground, and the wind was blowing. I questioned him about where his coat was and said, "Buddy, you must be freezing!"

He turned to me, completely straight-faced and announced, "Teacher, my people don't get cold!"

I smiled and questioned, "Your people, huh? Which people are those?"

He smiled and said, "My African brothers, we don't get cold!"

I said, "Really? Tell me about that."

He said, "My people come from where the sun always touches the earth, and we are warmed from the inside out, so we never get cold."

I said, "Wowzers, that is fascinating. Thanks for sharing that information with me." He was very proud and shared with the rest of the class, too. They were awed!

When he came in from recess, his teeth were chattering, and he was jumping up and down to keep warm. I asked him how recess worked out with no coat. He smiled and waved at me and stood by his desk to say the Pledge. He was still shivering.

Just before lunch, I called him over and told him I had just gotten a new coat for Christmas and it was super nice and warm. I told him that my coat didn't really get to go outside very often, so I was wondering if he wouldn't mind wearing it to help me break it in. I asked him if he thought his "people" would mind. He was literally beaming. He said he would be happy to help me out with my coat and that he knew how hard it was to break in a new coat because he used to have to do that when he wore coats. I let him know how much I appreciated it. It was too big for him, but I could tell how grateful he was. He wore it for the next two weeks every day. He really helped me break it in. I told him how much I appreciated his help.

Junior was a very delightful young man with a great sense of humor. One day, he came in from recess bawling. He was really upset. I sat down, and he crawled up on my lap. He was sobbing. I tried to calm him down. He was panting and trying to tell me what happened. He finally got out, "Teacher, Johnny called me black!" He put his head on my shoulder and cried. I asked Johnny to come over and talk to me so that I could understand what had happened.

Johnny shuffled over. He thought he was in trouble but wasn't sure why. I told him he wasn't and that I just needed to know what happened. Johnny took a deep breath and said, "We were playing football with some kids from the other classes. I yelled to Jake and told him to pass it to the black kid because Jake doesn't know his name because he was in the other class." He was talking so fast it was hard to understand him. He continued, "I don't know why he got so mad. I wasn't trying to be mean. I thought he knew he was black."

Junior howled again, "See, he called me black!"

Johnny shrugged his shoulders and said, "I wasn't trying to be mean! I am really sorry, Junior. I want you to be my friend."

I told him that I knew he would never say anything mean on purpose and that I knew that they were friends. Johnny and I were both kind of stumped about the situation. I asked him to let me talk to Junior and see if I could figure out what had happened.

Junior finally started to calm down. We did the Pledge, and while the kids were eating their snack, I talked quietly with Junior. I explained that we were all a little bit confused about why he was so upset, explaining that Johnny would never hurt his feelings on purpose.

He exclaimed, "Teacher, they think I'm black!"

I wasn't sure how to react, and I stumbled over my words, "Junior, um ... well, see ... um…I'm not sure how to tell you this but ... um, you actually are black!"

He said, "Oh no, not you, too!" and began to cry again. I took him onto my lap again and patted his back while he cried. I was completely confused! I had no idea what to say, so I just held him while he cried.

He finally calmed down. I asked him if he wanted to talk about it and explain to me why he was so upset so we could solve it. I wiped away his tears.

He finally said, "Miss Melanie, look at my arm. Clearly, I am not black. Teacher, can't you tell I am dark, dark brown." The light finally came on in my head.

"Oh, I get it! So, if Johnny had said 'Throw it to the dark brown kid,' you would have been okay with that?"

He nodded his head. "Of course!"

I said, "Well, we can easily solve this! You just need to teach him what is appropriate."

I called Johnny over and explained the situation. He patted Junior's shoulder and repentantly said, "Junior, I am really sorry I called you black. I didn't mean to hurt your feelings. From now on, I will call you dark brown, okay? Can we still be friends again please?"

Junior nodded his head, and they high fived and went on being best friends.

35

CHARLIE

Poverty is like a sleeping lion. Sometimes it's dormant, but ever present, quietly breathing down one's neck. Then, occasionally, it springs into action and can be debilitating and render a person completely helpless.

Several years ago, I took a graduate class called Understanding Poverty that was offered through our school district. The class was fascinating, and I learned so much about the families in our area and the children I work with every day. It changed my mindset and how I teach.

I finally understood that there are two distinct kinds of poverty. The first kind is situational poverty. It's when a family is working hard, but because of certain factors, there is just not enough money. For instance, a lack of education can make it so the parents can't get a well-paying job, but they work hard to compensate by going to school and working or working extra jobs or overtime. They are trying to make their situation better.

The difference is pronounced in their children. In general, children of situational poverty are clean, and their hair is usually combed, teeth brushed, and their clothes, though older and ragged, are clean and tidy. You can usually tell that the family is struggling, but that the child is cared for.

The second type of poverty is generational poverty. These parents were usually raised in poverty, and their parents were raised in poverty, too, It goes back for generations. It seems they have accepted their lot in life. Their place in society and their plan is for others to take care of them. They believe that the government needs to provide for them because that is how poor people in America survive. It's owed to them because they were born. What I have noticed, however, is that children of generational poverty are usually filthy, dirty, and unkempt. Their clothes are dirty, and they wear the same clothes day after day. Their faces and hair have not been washed for days, sometimes weeks. They don't know how to or won't brush their teeth. I think the parents think someone needs to come into their home and take care of their kids. No matter how much help they get in food stamps or welfare, it's never enough.

At Christmas time, these children's names are put on every Secret Santa and church and charitable gift list so they can receive gifts from all organizations who provide Christmas for the poor. I taught a little girl who lived with her grandma. After Christmas, she told us about all of the presents she had received. She got an MP3 player, an iPad, a Kindle, three pairs of designer jeans, a fancy new coat, Air Jordan basketball shoes, a Wii, and seven games.

She announced to the class that "it's good to be poor because you get everything you want." She told me privately that her grandma was really good at "playing the system" and getting her everything she wants for Christmas. Her grandma calls all of the organizations who provide free stuff to poor kids and gives them her name and tells them what she wants. She also told me that her grandma lets her choose which gifts she wants to keep the most, and then they return the rest to the stores to get cash so her grandma can get what she wants. I thought, *Wowzers, people work hard for that money and out of the goodness of their hearts try to help you have a wonderful Christmas,* but to her and her grandma, it was just a racket to rake in cash.

She also told me that some of the items she didn't want were sold to their friends for cash, too. I was flabbergasted, but then figured out a lot of families did the same thing. I have often thought that there should be some kind of clearinghouse where the different charities talk to each other so that everyone in need can have a good Christmas and all of their resources aren't spent on the same few families who know how to work the system.

Charlie was a little blonde, blue-eyed child. I had taught four of her five siblings. I knew that their mother was the queen of generational poverty. We fed all her children breakfast and lunch, and they were all on the backpack program and took home bags of food every Friday. The mom had already told me that she didn't know how to read or write and that she hated math, so I was not to expect any help with school work at home. She also told me that she was too busy to help her kids and that I should not bother her to ask for help. She told me that she had her first baby the day she turned 14, and every time she needed more money from the government, she had to have another baby.

Charlie was her sixth baby, and she was getting too tired to have any more. She also told me that her three oldest boys were all in trouble with the law. The oldest was in prison, and the other two were in juvy and that they were all "good for nothings" just like their fathers. She did, however, have hope for her three girls because they were so pretty that they might be able to catch them a husband someday. Yup, I was in shock. I didn't even know what to say to her.

Charlie was a watcher. She watched everything. She watched the kids to see what they were doing all the time. She got good at copying other children's work. Her copying skills were amazing. I would try to work with her and tell her she didn't need to copy the other kid's work because she was smart enough to do the work on her own. I told her I would help her. She would shake her head and go back to watching the other kids. She stared at people, which would make them feel uncomfortable. The kids would ask me to ask her to stop staring at them. Her reaction was always the same: "I'm not staring at them. I'm just watching." It was very weird.

Charlie always had a dirty face and dirty hair. She told me that she took one bath per week with her two sisters except on weeks when their water was turned off. Sometimes, she told me they bathed in the hose in the front of their trailer. She said she didn't like soap that much — that it got in her eyes, and so she wouldn't use it. Her mom was often reluctant to wash their hair because they didn't have any shampoo because it cost too much money, so I sent home a bottle of shampoo.

Of course, I tried to get them more help, but our school social worker said that she couldn't keep up with all the mother's requests and the children's needs, and then she found out their mom was selling the stuff she was giving them to get money. Our social worker was frustrated with the whole family. It seemed the more she helped, the more they needed and expected and the less it was appreciated.

Health and Welfare was well aware of this family and had been for years and years. They were doing all they could to help them, too, but whatever help it was, it was never enough. They played the system like a finely tuned fiddle.

One day, we were going on a field trip that would cost 50 cents for each child. Charlie's mom wrote me a note and said Charlie couldn't go on the field because she didn't have 50 cents for her and that she didn't have a boyfriend to help pay either. She said Charlie could stay at school with her sister while we all went on the field trip. Of course, I paid the 50 cents. I thought Charlie would have been embarrassed, but she just grabbed the money from me and paid. There was no thank you, no appreciation at all.

We were working on a project based around families and how many different kinds of families there are. I explained that anyone who loved and cared about them could be considered family. We knew that some kids lived with grandparents or aunts and uncles. Some kids just lived with their mom, some kids went back and forth between their mom's and dad's homes, and some kids had a mom and a dad that lived at the same home. We talked about how some kids have step-parents, too, and some even have parents that are the same gender. I explained that there are all different kinds of families, but that everyone belonged to a family. The kids were writing about their families and drawing pictures. It was truly fascinating. Times have changed so much since I was a kid.

Charlie came up to me and showed me her picture. She had drawn her mom hugely in the middle and all her tiny siblings around her. She drew her brother in jail and everyone else sitting around on couches. She said, "Teacher, I don't know which dad I should draw." I asked her to explain. She said, "Well, I have five dads. My sister has dad number four. My other sister has a dad. He is number three and he is my favorite because he is nice, and he pays my mom money for her. Two of my brothers have the same dad, but he is a bum and is in jail. My biggest brother had dad number one, and he pays money, too. My real dad is number five, but we don't even know where he is anymore. I have lots of uncles, too, but my mom doesn't marry them. She only gets married when she wants to have a baby so they can give her money. Do I have to draw dad number five? I don't like him the most because he hitted my mom too much."

She went on and on about all her dads and uncles and men who had lived in their trailer with them. My jaw dropped. I was in shock, but she just kept right on talking. I asked myself, *How does a 7-year-old already have five dads?* I wasn't sure what to say to her, so I told her to draw the dad that made her feel the happiest and was the nicest to her. She said she was going to choose dad number three because he called her Charlie Brown and smiled at her and brought her candy when he came to see her sister, and sometimes, she even got to ride in his car. And, she told me, he was the only dad who had a job, so he had some money. She told me that he gave her sister new clothes, and sometimes, her sister even let her wear some of them when they got too little for her.

She told me that her dad was number five and that her mom called him the "biggest loser of all" because he wouldn't pay any child support, so she didn't get to see him ever, which was fine with her because he was "creepy." I honestly didn't know what to say to her. I was speechless. I just hugged her and finally said, "Wowzers, you have one amazingly, interesting family, Charlie Brown!" She giggled.

It hurt my heart to listen to this little girl go on and on about how dysfunctional her family was. She told me that, sometimes, her mom would leave them for the whole weekend to go find a new boyfriend and make some money, so they had to take care of themselves. She said that, sometimes, one of her brothers would come home, but that they were really mean to her and her sisters and that they would pull their pants down and spank their bare bums. The situation was horrible. I kept calling social services and they already knew and would send someone to their trailer, but nothing ever changed.

Social services were aware of this family. I was told that the mom knew all of the rules and knew exactly how to do just enough to keep the kids from being taken away from her. Charlie told me that her mom had to keep them because she needed the money. The mom even asked me to babysit once so she could go on a trip with her new boyfriend. I told her that that wasn't possible, as I needed to care for my own children and that I thought she needed to take care of hers. She acted really hurt that I would even make that kind of suggestion.

Academically, Charlie was very low. She couldn't read and didn't really care if she learned. She told me once that she didn't need to know how to read and that her mother didn't know how to read. She was just going to grow up and have babies so the government would give her money, just like her mother. She had no ambition to work towards a better life. I tried and tried to show what she could be. I explained that she could be anything she wanted to be if she would learn to read and do math and work hard. I told her that I believed in her and that she was beautiful and kind and smart and that I was excited to see how great she was going to turn out. She just stared at me. I asked her what her goals in life were. She told me that someday she wanted to go shopping at Walmart. She had heard it was awesome and amazing and someday she was going to go there. She told me she wanted to go there to watch people because she thought that would be interesting.

I tried everything I could think of to get her to set her sights higher. I explained that if she worked hard in school she could be a teacher or a police officer or a judge or a nurse or a doctor or a social worker and help kids.

She thought for a minute and finally said, "Do you think maybe I could grow up and work at Walmart?"

I excitedly said, "Yes, but you have to learn how to read and do math and graduate from high school. That would be a great career choice for you, but you'd have to work really hard and show them how smart you are! You can do it. I know you can!"

She just stared at me. I could tell she was thinking about what I had said. Finally, she just shook her head and said, "Never mind!" and walked away.

I tried to keep in touch with Charlie over the next several years. I really wanted her to make a better life for herself. She came back to visit me when she was thirteen. She told me she had dropped out of school because it was too hard and that she was having a baby so she could get some money from the government. She said her mom wasn't excited about being a grandma, but she was excited about the money they'd be getting from the government. She did thank me for making her learn to read because that had helped her a lot. She told me her baby's dad was nineteen and that he had dropped out of school, too. She said her mom wouldn't let him live with them unless he got a job and paid her some rent. (I was trying not to freak out. Seriously, a 19-year-old with a 13-year-old!? Really? He should be in jail!)

She thanked me for caring about her and said she was going to bring the baby to see me when he was born and, hopefully, I would have him when he was in second grade. Unsure what to do or say, I just hugged her and told her I cared about her and asked if she was sure she didn't want to give the baby up for adoption. I told her that she could be a good mother, but that it was a lot of work. I said to try to keep the baby clean so he would be a little healthier. I told her if she ever needed anything to call me and let me help. She stared at me, hugged me again, and walked out of my room.

After she left, I sat down and cried. My heart hurt for her and especially for that little baby. Another generation born into poverty.

36

CHEVY

From the first day I met Chevy, I knew he was troubled. He refused to look me in the eyes or even look at me at all. He could not focus on anyone or anything. He seemed to be in a world of his own. I have worked with many students that I would say have an attention deficit, but Chevy was different. If you asked him a direct question, like, "What is your name?" he would yell, "Blood is blue," and run away. Or if you would ask, "Would you like a snack?" he would screech, "Puppies should die!" It was very strange. I would try to get him to sit with the group, but he would ignore me and refuse to join us at all. If I touched him, he would freak out. He would scream and kick and then run.

One of the most interesting things about Chevy was how fearless he was. He was reckless. At recess, he would climb to the top of the monkey bars and then dive off like he was trying to fly. He would crash to the ground, but even when he was hurt, he would jump up and do it again. He would ignore us when we tried to get him to stop and explain to him that it was very dangerous. I felt completely invisible to him. He totally tuned us out.

He would ask the other kids to hit him in the face. The kids would look at me, and I would shake my head. The other children would obey, but it would make Chevy mad. He would yell, "Come on, Teacher. Just let 'em hit me!" I tried to explain to him that I can't just let kids hurt him. He would say, "They can't even hurt me. I am Superman!"

If I turned my back on him at all, he would climb on top of the table or my desk or whatever was the highest point in the room. Once, he tried to climb on top of file cabinets and jump off before I caught him. He could have easily broken a bone. I tried and tried to talk to him about it and explain how easily he could get hurt. He honestly didn't care.

Chevy was such an interesting child. He had light-brown skin and dark brown eyes. He had a buzz cut hairdo around the back of his head but the hair on the top of his head was long and curly and brown. He was tall and very thin.

I was at a loss as to how to help little Chevy. He didn't hurt the other kids; he usually didn't even notice the other kids. Most of the other students just stared at him trying to figure out what he was going to do next.

The kids asked me a lot of questions about Chevy. "Why is he so weird?" was the most popular question. "Why does he try to hurt himself all of the time?" "Do you think he really thinks he can fly?" I tried as hard as I could to answer their questions, but I was stumped and confused as well.

Our school district psychiatrist, counselor, and principal tried to help our class, but they had never seen a case like Chevy before either. They advised me to teach the other kids and to just try to manage Chevy the best I could. He was very disruptive and acted completely unaware that anyone else was even in the room.

One day, Chevy was crawling under and over the desks and trying to fly from one desk to another. I had to insist that he get down, which really upset him. He crawled under a table that was pushed against a corner in our room. I was hoping he would be safe for a few minutes while the other kids were working. We had about ten minutes until recess.

As the students started preparing to go outside, I heard Chevy yelling, "Hey you guys, hit the table really hard!"

To my horror, I saw that Chevy had pushed the table far enough away from the wall to get his head out and was hanging from his chin. He had lifted himself off the ground. The table was pushed against his throat. He wanted the kids to run into the table. He was shouting, "You guys can cut my head off if you want to!"

Unfortunately, one of the little boys in my class, who was not actually a little kid at all, was happy to answer Chevy's request because he was constantly annoyed by him. He was thrilled to oblige. He started to run as fast as he could towards the table. I dove over a desk and two chairs and barely grabbed his shirt in time to stop him.

Chevy yelled, "Aw, Teacher, I told him to. I want to get my head cut off today!"

We had a hard time getting Chevy's mother to respond to our requests for help. When we could finally get her to answer her phone or call us back, she would say she would come to the school to talk to us, but she wouldn't show up when we set up meetings. It was so frustrating because no one really knew what we were dealing with.

Chevy was new to the school, and we had no history about him. We had requested his file from his former school, but were told he had been home schooled, so there was no information. Mom was in the process of trying to get government help, so she had to put him in school.

One day, I asked Chevy if he would like to eat lunch with me. He answered, "Bad guys should die, and so should I."

I said, "Okay, I'll tell you what: I will walk the whole class down to the lunch room. Then after you get your lunch, if you want to come back and eat with me, you can."

He had no response. I couldn't even tell if it registered or if he even understood me.

I shrugged my shoulders and said, "Chevy, I'd love it if you would be my lunch buddy today, but it's up to you."

Once again, nothing!

I walked the kids down the hall to the lunch room and returned to my classroom to eat. Several minutes later, I heard a noise outside of my room. It was like a muffled siren sound. I walked to the door, and Chevy was sitting on the floor outside my room with his lunch. His hands were covering his mouth, and he was squealing like a siren.

I said, "Chevy, I am so glad you came back to eat with me. Do you want to come in and sit at the table with me?"

No response.

I asked again. Nothing!

I finally went in and grabbed my sandwich and went into the hall and sat across from him. I said, "We can just eat together if you want. Or we can talk about stuff if you want." He started eating. We sat in silence for a long time.

Finally, he spoke.

"Teacher, do you know I killed my sister? The fired house fell on her, and she got dead." He kept on chewing and wouldn't look at me.

I choked and coughed and gasped and finally was able to say, "I'm sorry, what did you say?" There was a long, long pause. I said, "Would you like to tell me about it?"

No response.

I tried not to stare at him. I didn't know what to think. He had said so many really strange things in the past, so I wasn't sure if I should believe him. I was perplexed. We sat for a long, long time.

Finally, he said, "Superman can't get dead in a fire even if the house falls down!" He got up, grabbed his tray and walked to the lunch room to dump it and ran outside. I sat there for a long time until another teacher questioned me about sitting alone in the hall.

After school, I tried to call his mom again. I left a message explaining what Chevy had said and begging her to please contact the school so we could get him some help. I know I sounded desperate, but I was at a loss as to how to help this little boy who believed he could fly.

Several days later, Chevy's mom showed up at the school just as the bell rang at the end of the day. She introduced herself. She was very, very thin with long, stringy hair. The first thing I noticed as she talked was how rotten her teeth were. I was so struck by her appearance that I fumbled for words.

She said, "Okay, here is the damn story. My old man was cooking meth. He was a real son-of-a-bitch, but he was paying the bills. One night, I left the kids home and went out. He was high on sh** and out of his mind and set the G**damn house on fire. He got out and passed out on the front lawn.

"Our next-door neighbor saw the fire and called the f***ing fire department. They got there pretty fast, but the roof was on fire. One of the fire dudes pulled Chevy out of the G**damn house before the roof fell in, so they couldn't get Missy out. Why the hell would he save that little piece of sh** and let my baby girl burn? They are a bunch of a**holes, I tell ya! Then they took my old man to jail, so how the hell am I supposed to pay the bills? My life sucks sh**!"

I literally just stared at her. I could not even form a sentence. After a few seconds, she went on, "You're not going to have to worry yourself no more about Chevy. We are moving so my mom can take care of him 'til I have this baby." She patted her stomach. "And I hope to hell it's a f***in' little girl! This Friday is that little piece of sh**'s last day, and we won't be bothering you no more."

Then she walked out of the room.

I honestly felt like I had been run over by a truck. Every part of me hurt for that little boy. He had created some sort of alternate reality for himself so that he could cope. I knew that I could not be part of his world or even begin to try. I was heartbroken.

I contacted the necessary authorities to try to get this family some help, but I'm not sure anyone really knew what to do. I prayed that Chevy's grandma would be good and kind to him. I hoped they would get him some professional help. I didn't even want to think about the unborn child. I felt helpless and hopeless and grateful that Chevy had touched my life, but was devastated that I had had no effect on his. I knew I was unable to help and prayed with all my heart that someone, somewhere could save that little starfish.

37

CAMMIE

Cammie was a bright-eyed, happy-go-lucky little brownish-blonde haired 7-year-old. I felt lucky to have her in my class. From the first day of school, she was a joy. She loved to laugh, and she loved to learn. She was chatty and loved to visit with her neighbors and friends and strangers. In fact, after about two days, there were no more strangers. She had made everyone her friend.

She was one of those kids that just lit up a room when she walked in. She had an easy smile and gregarious personality. She assumed everyone liked her. "What's not to like, right?" she'd say.

And everyone did.

She would ask me every day, "So Teacher, what amazing, wonderful, fun things do you have planned for us to learn today?" She was a joy.

She was a good reader and a good student. She was quick to offer help to other kids who were struggling with anything. She was a good problem-solver and made sure everyone was included in any group games. No one was ever left out when Cammie was around. She was a gift to a hard-working teacher because she was very helpful and had a wonderful attitude.

Cammie shared with me that she lived with her mom because

her dad was in rehab because he had drug issues and that he had been in jail before. She said she had a little brother and sister, but they had a different mother and they were supposed to be with their dad because their mom took off because she didn't want anything at all to do with them anymore. Cammie whispered, "She has drug issues, too!"

Cammie was grateful for her mom because she knew she loved her and was happy that she took such good care of her. She worried about her younger siblings because they were now in foster care. Their dad was in rehab and couldn't take care of them. She explained that their dad's health wasn't very good and that she was a little worried about him, but he was getting taken care of in rehab. She spoke very matter-of-factly about the situation.

I could tell she was very fond of her siblings and wanted to help them somehow, but felt unable to do anything for them. Apparently, their foster parents let the kids get together a few times a month. She would tell me when they all got to visit how cute and adorable they were. Jonah, her brother, was two years younger than her, and Peggy was two years younger than him.

As the year progressed, it was a pleasure to watch Cammie learn and grow and giggle and love life. She was so bubbly and joyful that the other kids were drawn to her, and she was constantly surrounded by lots and lots of friends. She was a kind and loving person.

Shortly before Christmas, Cammie told me that she was going to get to see her dad at Christmas because he was going to get out of rehab and her siblings were going to go back to live with him. She was super excited to get to see her whole family on Christmas day. She said her dad probably wouldn't get them any presents because he never did, but she couldn't wait to see her little brother and sister. She had saved up her classroom money and bought presents for her dad, her mom, and her little brother and sister at the class store and was bursting with excitement to give the carefully wrapped gifts to them on Christmas day.

After Christmas, when Cammie came back to school, something

was different. She was not the joyful little sunshine girl I knew and loved. She was much more solemn to the point that I thought she was quite moody. She became very quiet and started to push friends away. She spent much more time by herself. We teachers are conditioned to look for signs of abuse by noticing significant changes in personality and behavior. I immediately reported my concerns to our school counselor, who visited with Cammie.

After their visit, Cammie wanted to talk with both the counselor and me together and explained that over the Christmas holiday she had been able to spend a lot of time at her father's tiny apartment. She said, "My dad is a hot mess."

She confided that he was sick all the time and just lay around and slept and moaned. She ended up taking care of her little brother and sister. She had noticed that Jonah spent a lot of time trying to take care of their dad, but that their dad just yelled at Jonah a lot and was really mean to him. She was so worried about Jonah and Peggy because Cammie was now back with her mom and no one was really taking care of her siblings. (Her dad had gotten custody of the little kids when he got out of rehab because their mother had left the state and was no longer involved in their lives at all.)

Cammie was pacing back and forth and wringing her hands. With tears in her eyes, she pleaded, "I don't know how to help them now. What should I do? They are so little and helpless. Jonah thinks he is Mr. Tough Guy, but he is just a little kid. I am so worried. What should I do?"

She seemed to have the weight of the world on her little shoulders. It truly hurt my heart to see the grief in her face and the sorrow in her eyes. Her whole body shook with worry.

I took her in my arms and tried to calm her down. She was shaking and close to tears. We assured her that we were going to help and that we were impressed with her concern and care about her siblings and that she was a wonderful gift in their lives. I told her how grateful we were that she shared her feelings with us so that we could help. She melted into tears and sat weeping on my lap. Her little tender heart was broken.

The counselor immediately contacted Child Protective Services and explained what was happening. Our counselor was put in touch with the children's assigned case worker. The case worker was aware of the situation, and they were trying to get help for the dad and the kids. She appreciated Cammie's input and would help as much as she could.

After this experience, Cammie's behavior became a pattern. Every Monday, after she had spent the weekend with her dad and siblings, she fretted about their situation. She would say, "I think my dad is going to die today. I hope someone helps Jonah and Peggy. I am pretty sure he is going to die today!" She explained that the drugs had ruined his liver and that they made him really sick and that he would probably die soon. He had told her this over and over again, and that is why he needed her to help with Jonah and Peggy. She was tortured by the fact that she could only help them on the weekends.

When we checked in with their social worker, she told us they were getting help for the dad when he would let them and that he still had custody of the little ones. I tried to assure Cammie of this. By Wednesday each week, she would start to feel better and start to focus back on her school work. The bright-eyed, happy-go-lucky little girl was gone. There was no more giggling, no more directing groups or helping other kids. She worked hard and was a very good student, but she was weighed down by concern and pain. By Friday, I would see a little glint of joy back in her eyes. She loved Fantastic Friday and tried to find the fun, as she put it. Then the weekend would come, she would go back to her dad's, and the pattern would start all over again.

Her mother, of course, was very concerned about the situation and had considered trying to cancel her weekend visits with her father, but Cammie had begged her not to because she felt so responsible for Jonah and Peggy. Her mom didn't really know what to do. Our counselor continued to work with Cammie to help her understand that taking care of the little kids was not her responsibility, but Cammie explained that she had a "special bond" with them and knew she could help them. We were all impressed with the maturity of this little girl and her ability to be empathetic in this horrible situation.

In March, we had Parent-Teacher Conference. These are wonderful 20-minute meetings where the teacher gets to visit with each child's parents and explain their child's strengths and successes in learning and ask for help in the areas in which their child is struggling. They are usually very positive and constructive meetings that benefit the child because it gets the parents and the teacher all on the same page.

The meetings last all day at 20-minute intervals and are usually scheduled back-to-back from 8:00 a.m. to 8:00 p.m. to allow us time to accommodate all the parents. It's an exhausting day, but meeting the parents provides insight into the behavior and habits of the children. It's also useful when the parents are willing to help at home to support their learning at school. Cammie's mom called me and asked if I would mind meeting with Cammie's dad in a separate conference then hers.

I said, "That is an interesting request because it's all about the same child, but of course I will."

She said, "You will understand why after you meet with him."

I said I could meet with him at 8:00 p.m. after I had met with all the other kid's parents. She was very grateful.

I had never met Cammie's dad, so when he showed up at school, unshaven and disheveled, and walked right into my room while I was still in a conference with another child's parents, I was shocked. I asked him to please wait outside because we were almost finished and he was a little early. He grumbled and leaned against the wall tapping his foot and cleaning his fingernails. I quickly finished with the parents, as his presence had made us all uncomfortable. They left as quickly as possible.

I stood up and walked over to Cammie's father and offered my hand and introduced myself and started to explain what a delightful and bright child Cammie was and how lucky he was to be her father. He instantly interrupted me and said he thought I got paid way too much money and he didn't understand the world because taxes shouldn't go to schools and teachers because he knows people who would teach his kids for free and they would be thrilled about it and teachers are useless and they just try and get him in trouble and he never does anything wrong and teachers just keep sending CPS to check on him but he takes good care of his kids.

I offered him a chair to sit on, but he just paced back and forth, ranting and raving. He started explaining how he had gotten mixed up in drugs when he was 13 because his older brother had given them to him, and now he was hooked, and he had to go to rehab or he would have to go back to jail. He went on and on about how horrible women had ruined his life and he had been married three times and all of the bitches had had kids and he didn't even think they were his and that his last bitch had dumped the damn kids on him and he loved them but he didn't really want to take care of them and that teachers can't and shouldn't expect him to help with their school work because that is their job not his and that he is too busy to work with his kids and what did they expect from a single dad.

It was shocking to listen to him go on and on. A few times, I tried to talk and turn the conversation back to Cammie, but he was not interested in anything I had to say. He went on and on and on. I'm not even sure what he was even ranting about some of the time. I tried to listen, but he jumped from subject to subject so quickly that, frankly, I gave up. It was easy to tell he had no interest in anything I had to say about his daughter.

I kept thinking about Cammie's mother's warning, "You will understand after you meet him."

Oh boy, did I ever understand now.

Finally, thank goodness, around 8:30 p.m. the principal came to check on me, as I was the only teacher still left in the building, and he rescued me. I truly think Cammie's father would have stayed there all night ranting about the evils of, well, everything. The principal shook his hand and put his arm on his shoulder and escorted him out of my room. He was very kind, but firm. Apparently, the principal had dealt with this father before. After they left, I felt like I had been hit by a truck. I was trying to process what he had said and trying to figure out how Cammie fit into all his mess and how I could help her. I was very shaken.

My conferences had gone great the whole day, and I had been so impressed with all the parents because I had gotten the sense that they really cared about their kids and their learning, until I got to the last one. What a difference!

The principal walked him all the way to his car to make sure he didn't return to my classroom. After he drove away, the principal came back to check on me. I was staring at the wall in shock. The meeting helped me understand the change in Cammie's behavior and the situation she was having to deal with. I was heartbroken for that little girl and her siblings. The principal thanked me for caring so much about these little kids and appreciated how much love and concern I have for them. I thanked him repeatedly for saving me. I brought him a cinnamon roll the next day. I believe if it hadn't been for the principal, I would probably still have been there in the morning listening to Cammie's dad go on and on and on.

I watched Cammie carefully for the rest of the year. The pattern continued. Mondays were horrible, but by Friday, her wonderful little personality would start to shine through, but come Monday, it started all over again. Her mother and I worked together as much as we could, and Cammie ended up being very successful with her education. I would have done anything to take away the worry and pain she suffered each week. She was a remarkable young lady who seemed to be carrying her entire family's problem all on her shoulders. I pray with all my heart that somehow, someway, someday Cammie will be able to get her sunshine back.

38

JONAH

From the first time I met Jonah, I knew he would change my life. He was a tiny little second grader, but he was tough as nails. He walked into my room on the first day of school and planted his feet firmly on the ground; his hands were balled as fists, and his arms were crossed over his chest.

"So," he said, "my sister Cammie says you're pretty cool, and I have to give you a chance, but I think you should know that I hate school, I hate learning, I hate teachers, I know I am going to hate you, and I know, for sure, that you're going to hate me. It's just a matter of time because I am trouble — I mean it. Big trouble."

He was so serious. He had a determined, angry look on his face and looked like he was ready for a fight. His teeth were clenched, and his gray-blue eyes flashed intense anger. Wowzers! I was speechless.

At first, I was shocked by him, but something deep down inside of me whispered, "You must learn to love this child. He needs you."

I sat next to him on the table so I could look him in the eye, and I forced myself to smile and say, "Well, Mr. Jonah, it's semi-nice to meet you. I am Ms. Melanie, and I would like to accept your challenge."

He almost smiled.

I continued, "I will bet you that, within three months, not only will you like school, but you will like me, and you will be one of my favorite kids I've ever taught."

I put my hand out to shake on it. "What do you say?' I asked.

He actually reached for my hand, and as we shook, he mischievously smiled and said, "There is no way that is going to happen, but game on, sister!"

Who knew that he would become one of the greatest challenges of my career?

Jonah was a runner. If things didn't go his way or there was a concept I was trying to teach that he didn't understand immediately, he would scream "This is stupid" and run out of the room. He would run down the hall and out of the building. Sometimes, he would run around the building, but usually, he would run through the neighborhoods surrounding the school. He didn't usually have a destination. He would just run until somebody found him. When they did, he was so angry that he would punch and scratch and try to bite.

Because I was unable to leave the rest of my students, someone else usually had to deal with his running, which made things so much worse. He hated to be touched and would become wild if he was restrained. Typically, it was the principal and the counselor who would have to go find him. They learned quickly not to touch him and just tried to calm him down so they could talk to him. No disciplinary action helped these events. They tried various disciplinary tactics, suspensions, and timeouts. Nothing really worked. Everything just made him angrier.

He almost won the bet. I was becoming so frustrated. I could not figure out how to manage, let alone, teach this kid. No punishment worked because that is what he longed for. He thrived on negative attention. He would yell at me, almost taunting me, "I told you I was a bad kid. See, I proved I'm a bad kid!"

It really became a torturous game for both of us.

I spent many long hours discussing Jonah with our school counselor, the principal, and even the school district's psychologist. We were at our wit's end. I will admit it: I prayed. I know it sounds desperate, but every night, I would kneel and beg for guidance on how to deal with and help Jonah. I had asked for Heavenly input with many of my students, but I *begged* for help with Jonah. I had felt so much anger and frustration with him that I knew I would fail if I didn't seek some kind of Divine inspiration.

Very clearly, an idea came to my mind with a spiritual peace that assured me it was right.

"Make him laugh. Make it a game."

I questioned, "Are you kidding? There is no way he is going to laugh. He is in so much pain and so full of anger. There is nothing I can do that is going to make him laugh."

Again, I got the intense feeling. "Make him laugh. Make learning a game."

To use a British term, I was "gob-smacked," but I was desperate. I thought and thought and prayed and prayed and pleaded to figure out what to do. I tried to prepare myself and felt inadequate, but willing to give it a try.

I was willing to try anything.

On Monday morning, as usual, Jonah stomped into the room and threw his backpack and jacket somewhere towards the vicinity of his coat hook. He knocked over several chairs and slammed himself into it his own. Honestly, I was scared, but I took a deep breath and said, "Jonah, will you please come and talk to me for a minute?"

He stomped over. "What do you want now?" he growled.

I said, "I was wondering if you know why the chicken crossed the road?"

He screeched, "What?"

I said again, "I was just wondering if you knew why the chicken crossed the road." He just looked at me like I had lost my mind.

I said, smiling, "To get the other side!" He crossed his arms and just stared at me.

I took another deep breath and said, "Now, do you know why

the duck crossed the road?" I looked at Jonah, hopefully. He put his hands on his hips, but seemed to be anticipating an answer.

I said, "Okay, well the duck crossed the road because the chicken was on vacation."

Nothing!

He just stood there, staring at me. I felt self-conscious. It seemed like an hour passed, but I am sure it was just a few seconds. I blew out a long, long breath, thinking, "I know it was a really dumb joke, but I prayed that it would work."

Slowly, very slowly, I noticed a little tiny smile start at the corners of his mouth.

Finally, he said, "Teacher, that is the stupidest thing I've ever heard." But he laughed, kind of a disgusted, exasperated laugh as he rolled his eyes and stomped back to his seat. I wasn't sure what had just happened, but I did know I had given humor (yes, as bad as it was) a try.

The day went on as usual. I tried not to make him mad or push him too hard, and he only ran once. By now, the principal was on call and dealt with the situation the best she could. There was constant tension whenever we dealt with Jonah. He was so unpredictable; we never really knew what to expect and what would set him off. I was always grateful for the end of the day when I knew we had made it through with no injuries and no calling the police to help us get him back to school. Any day that didn't involve the police was a success.

However, this day was different. At the end of the day, after the bell had rung, Jonah came up to me and said, "So, Ms. Melanie, why did the wolf cross the road?"

I was stunned, but tried to hide my shock. "Um, um. I don't know, Jonah. Why did the wolf cross the road?" For the first time in our lives together, I saw a little sparkle in his eyes.

He yelled, "So he could eat the stupid duck and the chicken!" He wailed with laughter. It was the first time I had ever heard him laugh. I was so shocked by his laughter that it took me a minute to get the joke. He was laughing so hard that it made me laugh, and by the time I got the joke, it was hysterical. I knew from that second on I that had broken through. This was not the same angry, venomous boy I had met a month before.

I said to him as he was running out the door, "Thanks, Jonah. You made my day." He was gone, but he left laughing.

Every day after that, I was armed with some corny joke. I would like to personally thank the Boy Scouts of America Handbook for printing the dumbest jokes on earth, but they worked. In the morning, I would tell Jonah some dorky joke, and at the end of the day, he would figure out how to make the joke better.

I would say, "Knock, Knock." He would say, "Who's there?" I would say, "Harry." He would say, "Harry who?" I would say, "Harry up, it's cold out here." He would roll his eyes and skip back to his seat, but I could tell the wheels were spinning.

At the end of the day, he would say to me, "Hey, Teach. Knock, knock."

"Who's there?"

"Harry."

"Harry who?"

"Harry up, Teacher, I need to go home!"

He would laugh, I would laugh, and then he would skip to the bus and tell his friends the jokes.

On another day, I said, "Hey, Jonah. Why did the cookie go to the doctor? Because he was feeling crumby." He would smile and roll his eyes, but at the end of the day, he asked, "Hey Teacher. What did the doctor say to the crumbs?" 'Cake' a pill and call me in the morning." He was so clever. He actually started to act like he didn't totally hate school.

One day, I took a risk:

"Knock, Knock."

"Who's there?"

"Jonah."

"Come on. Okay, Jonah who?"

"Jonah a good dentist? I got a bad tooth."

At first, he just stared at me, and I wondered if I had hurt his feelings using his name to make a joke. Then he smiled and said, "Teacher, knock, knock."

I hesitantly asked, "Who's there?"

He laughed and said, "Jonah thinks that joke is stupid!" We both laughed, and I realized I genuinely liked this kid. He was still a stinker most of the time, but I felt like we were building a bridge.

Over time, I had begun to notice that if he didn't run, he would have full-on temper tantrums. He would kick and scream and scratch and bite and attack whoever was trying to deal with him. If he was stopped from leaving the room when he was mad, he would go under a desk and act like a wild, caged animal. He would growl and hiss at us. So, once again, after many prayers, I came up with a solution that had to have been divinely inspired because it was crazy.

I bought a stopwatch and told Jonah that when he got upset and ran out of the room that I was going to start the timer and keep track of how long he was gone. Then, if he would promise to come back, I wouldn't call the principal, and we would deal with the time when he got back and was ready to learn. He didn't love dealing with the principal because he felt she made things worse, so he agreed to my plan.

The first time this worked, we were learning about adjectives. He could remember what a noun and a verb was, but he couldn't remember what an adjective was. One of the kids was trying to help him and said, "An adjective is a word you use to describe a noun."

Apparently, he thought the child was talking down to him and screamed right in her face, "I'm not stupid, you know!"

He ran out of the room. I calmly started the stopwatch and went on teaching, worrying the whole time if I needed to call the principal, but remembered that I was going to try to hold up my end of the bargain.

Jonah came back exactly 7 minutes and 36 seconds later. He was out of breath, panting, and a bit sweaty, but he came in and sat down. I paused the stopwatch and said, "Welcome back, Jonah. It's good to see you," and went on teaching like he had never left. He ran one more time that morning when someone accidently knocked his book off his desk. I started the timer. He was gone for 4 minutes 15 seconds that time. But he came back.

As the kids were getting ready for lunch, I said to him, "Jonah, I am glad you came back and I didn't have to call the principal, but you owe me 11 minutes and 56 seconds of learning time, so will you please get your lunch and bring it back to the classroom so I can help you get caught up on what you missed?"

He screamed at me and said, "That is so stupid! I hate you! You're so stupid!"

I said, "While that may be true, I still need you to come back to make up the time."

He was spitting out "Stupid teacher, I hate you!" all the way down the hall, but he did come back. It took all the patience I could muster, but as he ate, I caught him up on the work he had missed.

As I listened to him try to figure out the information, it dawned on me that I think he might have dyslexia. I could tell he was trying to show me he was smart, but he was really struggling with reading and writing. I soon realized that he didn't know phonics well at all and had probably never been read to. It was obvious that he had huge holes in his learning.

At first, it was hard for me to give up my lunch time to help him, but then I realized I could eat with him while he ate and worked. I also worried that he would run on purpose to "have to" spend lunchtime with me, but his running time got shorter and shorter and less and less. He would usually run at least once per morning, so he would have to come in at lunch, but as he filled in the learning holes and became more confident in his knowledge, he ran less.

Eventually, he stopped running completely. He knew if he didn't understand something, he could ask me or one of the kids to help him. I noticed fairly quickly that he was bright and caught on very well. Before long, he needed very little academic help at all. He would still come in at lunch, but slowly, our lunch hours consisted of just visiting. Each day, he would open up a little more.

I hadn't known much about his life. I knew he was in foster care with his little sister. I had met his dad when I had Cammie, and I didn't think very highly of him. Jonah and Cammie had different mothers. Cammie's mother had taken her and let her spend very little time with her father. Jonah's mother had abandoned Jonah and his little sister and had chosen the world of drugs over him and his little sister. That was how he explained it to me. His dad had tried to take care of him, but had told Jonah that he was too hard and had given him and his sister to the state of Idaho, and now they were in foster care.

Each day, Jonah would tell me another story about life with his dad and sister. I was horrified. He would just start talking, and I would sit there listening, mesmerized and trying not to cry. He just shared his stories matter-of-factly, step by step. I was amazed at his recall.

The first story he told me started by his showing me a scar on his hand. "I got this," he explained, "when me and Peggy and my dad got to stay at the homeless shelter. Well, first, we were staying with my grandma, but she hates my dad because he is so mean to her, and he shouldn't have got out a knife, and I shouldn't have tried to grab it and cut my hand, but I didn't want him to hurt my grandma, and my grandma said he had to go, but he could leave Peggy and me there, but she was not going to deal with his drinking anymore. He screamed at her and said she was never getting his kids. So he drug us out of the house.

"We walked around for a long time and then found a homeless shelter and we stayed overnight there. It was really scary because I had to take care of Peggy because she was crying." When he paused, I asked him how old he was at the time, and he told me he had just turned 5.

He started to trust me and soon started to pour out his heart and soul to me. I tried hard not to overreact, but his stories were horrific. I actually ended up calling the homeless shelter and talking to the gentleman who managed it. I asked him about Jonah and his sister and dad, and he explained that he couldn't really give me any information because of their privacy policies. I understood that and knew I needed to bend the rules a little to see if I could understand Jonah better. I asked the manager if I could repeat some of the stories Jonah had told me because I was trying to help him and needed to know if his stories were true. The gentleman said, "Go ahead."

I told him what Jonah had told me. There was a long, long silence.

Finally, he said, "I am really glad you're trying to help that little boy. He is very damaged and, yes, the stories he is sharing with you are true." I thanked him and hung up. I felt like I had been punched in the stomach. Some part of me was hoping that he was making them up. I believe no child should ever have to go through what Jonah had told me about, but the stories continued.

Jonah would tell me how he, Peggy, and their dad had to leave the homeless shelter. He said they would walk around a lot, and sometimes, they would go and sit in a park. Their dad would try to find some medicine, which I quickly figured out was alcohol, but he explained to them that he always felt better after he had taken his medicine. Jonah finally began to understand that a little bit of medicine helped his dad feel better, but a lot of medicine made his dad really mean.

At night, they would go back to the shelter. The dad would put them in bed and sneak back out in search of some more medicine. If he found some, he would either come back a raging madman or fall asleep on the front porch or the lawn. If he wasn't in the bed next to him in the wee hours of the morning, Jonah would try to go find him to help him sneak back into the house before the headmaster would find out he had left. He would often find his dad passed out somewhere outside and would beg him to get up and would drag him back into the shelter. He also told me that he would do everything he could to not wake Peggy up because she was terrified of her dad when he was drunk.

As Jonah would tell these stories, he would stare off into space. His eyes would glaze over, his hands would be balled into fists, and he would tap his toe really quickly. It almost seemed like he was in a trance. He wouldn't look at me, and I tried never to interrupt him. He never cried. He almost seemed like a little robot. Every fiber of my being wanted to pick him up and rock him and hug him and tell him he was safe and that he was loved and that I cared about him so much, but I didn't dare. It was so obvious how much deep, deep pain there was there. Sometimes, when he was telling a story, he would tell it so fast that I didn't think he was even breathing. Other times, he would tell them, and all he would do was breathe. It was almost like he was hyperventilating. I was astonished at the experiences he had been through. He honestly sounded like an old man who had been through war. He was so very wounded. He was broken.

He told me of a particularly bad fight his dad was in with his grandma. They were screaming and throwing things at each other and breaking furniture.

Jonah said, "They were both so out of control that I ran. I ran and ran as far as I could away from my grandma's house. I wanted to run to the end of the earth. I wanted to run forever." He stopped and stared at the wall. He was breathing heavily like he had been running. He took some deep breaths and calmed himself down.

I finally asked, "What happened next?" He turned to me and spat out the answer, very annoyed.

"I cried, okay? I laid down on the grass of someone's house, and I cried. It seemed like I cried forever, and I was hoping I would die."

He sounded tortured.

"I think I fell asleep. Then I woke up really fast because I remembered Peggy. I had to go help Peggy. So I got up and ran back as fast as I could. I ran and I ran, and I finally got to the house. Everything was quiet except that I could hear Peggy crying. I ran into the house. Grandma was asleep on the couch. Dad was gone, and Peggy was sobbing on her bed. I picked her up and begged her to stop. Crying always made my dad so mad. I held her and tried to help her feel better. I got her a drink and then laid down with her, and I think we went to sleep.

"Don't you dare tell my dad I cried. Promise? Don't tell him I cried. Men don't cry," he snapped.

Every part of my soul hurt for this little boy. I was in such awe of him. He explained to me that every time he wanted to die he remembered that it was his job to take care of Peggy. He explained that he was the man of the house, and she was his responsibility. This little 7-year-old kid was a grown-up man with such a burden on his shoulders.

I never touched Jonah. After he would tell me the stories, I would want to hold him and soothe him so much. But something told me not to touch him. I would always thank him for telling me, and I would tell him how much it helped me understand him and what he was going through. I could tell he didn't want me to feel sorry for him. He said to me once very sincerely, "Ms. Melanie, it's tough to be the grown-up when you're just a little kid." He repeated that statement many, many times.

Curious as to how he and Peggy got into foster care, I asked him one day. He looked at me with fire in his eyes and spewed, "It was horrible. One night, my dad had put us to bed at the homeless shelter and had gone out to have a good time. I stayed awake all night. I finally heard him yelling at someone. I ran downstairs and outside and watched as my dad pushed another man down and hit him in the face. They were screaming and fighting, and then the other man got up and hit my dad with something right across the face. I screamed and ran to them, and the other man ran off.

"My dad was laying on the ground bleeding everywhere. His face was cut, his nose was bleeding, his hand was bleeding. I tried to help him up."

Once again, Jonah had this faraway look as he was telling the story. I hung onto every word. "I tried to help him up, but he was too big for me, so I kind of dragged him into the shelter. We stumbled up the stairs, and he passed out on the bed. I ran to the bathroom to get some towels because I knew the headmaster would be mad if my dad got blood all over the place. I looked in the mirror. I was covered with blood now, too. I got the towels wet and went back to try to clean up the mess. He was bleeding everywhere.

"As soon as I put the cold, wet towel on the cut on his face, he started moaning and yelling as loud as he could. That woke Peggy up, and she started to cry. He grabbed her and told her to 'shut the f*** up.' I grabbed Peggy from him, and he pushed me away.

"The door flew open, and the headmaster of the house turned on the light. Peggy and I were on the floor covered with blood, and Dad was on the bed yelling like a crazy man bleeding everywhere."

He paused for a moment and then looked at me. I think he had forgotten I was there. Then he said, "That is the most scared I have ever been in my life. Everyone else in the house was there by then. A lot of the people thought my dad had hurt us because we were covered with blood, but it was actually his blood. Someone called 911. They took my dad to the hospital and took Peggy and me to the police station. We sat there for a while, and then a lady came and got us and took us to another lady at a house, and she gave us a bath and some food, and then we went to bed. I was so tired I didn't even wake up until dinner time. When I did wake up, I couldn't find Peggy, and I started to scream.

"The nice lady came in and said, 'It's okay, Jonah. She is in here playing with some toys. Would you like something to eat?'

"She smiled at me. I checked on Peggy and saw that she was safe. I looked all around the house. It was so nice and so clean. I remember sitting down at the table and starting to ask her a hundred million questions, like 'Where is my dad?' 'Who lives at this house?' 'Why are you so nice to us?' 'What is going to happen to us?' 'Are we in trouble?'

"She calmly answered all my questions one by one. She said she didn't know about my dad yet and that she was the emergency home for the foster care program and that they were going to find a nice house for us to go stay at for a while. She said that she was impressed because I was a very brave boy because I had tried to help my dad and protect my sister. She said not very many 7-year-olds could be that brave. She made me feel a lot, lot better."

It was time for the rest of the kids to come back in from lunch. I asked Jonah if he would tell me the rest of the story tomorrow. I told him that he didn't have to run to be able to come in and talk to me.

"Good, I am kind of getting tired of running," he said.

The next day, he told me about getting taken to Trisha and Kevin's house and that they were going to help them until their dad was ready to take care of them again. He told me that Trisha was nice, but that he tried to stay away from Kevin. When I asked him why, he said because he was mad all the time.

One day, I got a strong impression that I needed to encourage Jonah to write down his stories. I bought him an awesome journal. When I explained it to him, I said, "Jonah, I truly think you need to write down the things that have happened to you. Grown-ups don't understand how kids feel about the things that affect them. You have an amazing story to tell, and I really feel like you could be a voice for kids and help a lot of them and maybe even some grown-ups."

He smiled and asked, "Do you really think people would want to know what I have to say?"

I responded, "I really, really do. It's very rare to have a child who is so articulate and has such a good memory. It would be a bestseller."

He said, "I am going to pretend that I know what articulate means and think it's a good thing and, yes, Ms. Melanie, I will write a book." I explained what articulate meant, and he is now writing a book.

During the year I taught Jonah, my daughter was expecting my second grandchild. I had tried repeatedly to prepare Jonah for the fact that I was going to miss school for a week so that I could help with the new baby. He would just stare at me and walk away. It was a different reaction than I had expected. I thought he would argue or say he didn't care or something, but there was no reaction at all.

By then, he had stopped running and had become part of our classroom team. He had friends in the class and seemed to act almost like he had no cares in the world at all. He was thriving, and I told him all the time how impressed I was with how hard he worked and how smart he was. I promised him that I would be back after one week and that I wanted to hear more stories. He had no reaction and would just walk away.

The day finally came. My daughter called me and said she was in labor, so I headed to her home, which is a 3.5-hour drive away. It was a Wednesday, and I planned on returning the following Wednesday. I had tried to prepare my substitute for Jonah, but he was doing so well that I wasn't sure what to say.

I guess the first day went well. Then the second day, she started to teach them something Jonah wasn't familiar with, and he yelled, "I don't get this. This is stupid!" He ran out of the room, down the hall and disappeared into the neighborhood. One of the other kids explained to the stunned substitute that he did that sometimes and that she needed to call the principal. She did, and the principal rounded him up and talked to him and tried to calm him down. It was a rough couple of days, but they made it through.

On Monday, all Hell broke loose. Apparently, Jonah thought I would be back, and when the substitute brought the kids in from recess, he bolted again. This time, he was out of control, and they ended up having to call the police. The principal explained that he had completely become undone and wouldn't even talk to anyone. She called me at my daughter's house and begged me to come home early. I checked with my daughter. Her mother-in-law was coming the next day and said to go. (My wonderful daughter has become used to the affection and caring I have for my students and is very supportive of me.)

After the bell rang on Tuesday morning, I went to pick up the kids. At first, Jonah was really glad to see me, but then a dark cloud came over him, and he became very angry. He wouldn't talk to me. He wouldn't come to lunch with me. He ignored me all day. I kept telling him that I was very glad to see him. I showed all of the kids pictures of my new baby granddaughter, but Jonah refused to even look at the pictures. He was very angry with me. I decided to let it go until he was ready to talk. He completely ignored me for the rest of the week.

The next Monday, he walked into the classroom, hung up his coat and backpack, and sat in his chair like he was the saddest person on earth. I asked him to come talk to me. Honestly, I was scrambling for something to say.

Finally, I said, "Knock, knock!"

He looked at me and said, "Really?"

I said, "No, knock, knock."

"Okay, fine, who's there?"

"Lettuce."

"Lettuce who?" he said, exasperated.

I smiled and said, "Lettuce in, it's cold out here!" He stared at me for a minute, and then he shook his head, laughed and walked back to his desk and said, "Man, teacher. That was stupid."

My little Jonah was back!

I asked him to come and have lunch with me that day. He said "No," but then he showed up anyway. I explained to him that I was really sorry I was gone for a few days and that I missed him a lot. He wouldn't talk to me, but I could tell he was listening. There was a long pause. Finally, I started to tell him about my new granddaughter and how amazing she was and how much I loved her and how happy I was with her.

He put his head down on the table. I wasn't sure what to do, so I stopped talking. We sat in silence for a long time. He finally whispered something, but I didn't understand. I explained that I couldn't hear him and asked if he would he please say it again.

He whispered again.

I still couldn't understand what he said. I asked him again. He whispered louder this time, and I heard, "I didn't think you were coming back!"

I said, "I am so sorry. I told you I was coming back. I care too much about you to not come back. I am so sorry!" He still had his head down on the table and was shaking it.

He said, "No, you don't really understand. I didn't think you were ever coming back because of me."

I was shocked. "What, why? Why would I not come back because of you? I love you; I care about you. I was excited to see you, Jonah. You matter to me."

We sat there for a long, long time. I finally put my hand on his back. I had never touched him before, but I felt down deep that I needed to pat his back to reestablish our connection. He didn't flinch; he just sat there.

Finally, he lifted his head, and with tears rolling down his cheeks, he looked me in the eyes and said, "You just don't get it, Ms. Melanie, I am a throwaway kid!" and walked right out of the room.

My heart broke that day.

39

KEVIN & TRISHA

During the time that Jonah was in my class, CPS had taken custody away from his and Peggy's dad and placed them in a foster home. Their new "fake parents," as Jonah called them, were named Kevin and Trisha. They had moved from the Midwest and were delightful, kind people. I greatly admired them for being willing to take on the task of caring for Jonah and Peggy.

Trisha visited my room to discuss Jonah and asked how she could help. She said they had a lot of problems with him at home, but that they were determined to stick with it to help make their little lives better. She was so calm as she told me about the crazy behavior Jonah was displaying. She knew he was testing them, but she was convinced that if she loved him enough she could help. She tried to read with him and help him complete his homework. She said it was a struggle every time, but she was not giving up, no matter what.

I knew that what Jonah needed the most was consistency. He needed people he could rely on and who cared about him. He was so full of anger and did everything in his power to push people away. Trisha and I made plans about how we would work together to help this little boy make it through the year. She would address any issues we had at school, and I would explain how lucky he was to be with such good, stable people who cared about him.

It was quite amazing to watch Jonah's improvement — especially in his learning and his behavior as he worked through his troubles. Trisha was so kind and loving, and Jonah noticed immediately. He had never had that in his life, and he flourished under her care.

To Jonah, however, Kevin was another story. Kevin was a very kind, hard-working man. He was the kind of guy you know you can count on. In fact, he was a remarkable man. The problem was that he was a man. Jonah had no respect for men, especially men who he felt had power over him. Jonah was downright nasty to Kevin. Whenever he would even talk about Kevin, he would ball his hands into fists and plant his feet on the ground. His whole body would become tense.

During some of our lunches, I would ask Jonah about Kevin, and he would explain things to me like "He expects me to pick up my clothes and make my bed and pick up towels and empty the dishwasher and whatever else he can think of to torture me."

Honestly, I laughed. I didn't mean to, but I was expecting him to tell me something horrible about Kevin and how he treated him. Jonah told me that Kevin wouldn't let him take care of Peggy. When I asked him what that meant, he told me that Kevin said I need to worry about myself and that he and Trisha would take care of Peggy. He informed me that Kevin didn't understand that taking care of Peggy had been his job for years. He felt that Kevin had no right to tell him what to do and that he could take care of both Peggy and himself.

He also told me that Kevin wanted him to do sports and that he would throw a football to him and was teaching him to play basketball and baseball. When I said that I thought that was wonderful, he growled at me and said that he gets too mad because he can't do any of it and sports are stupid and Kevin is stupid and all dads are stupid. I realized that, no matter what Kevin did, Jonah was going to fight him every step of the way. I was super impressed that Kevin was even willing to fight the fight because I knew it was going to be a long battle.

In March, we had parent-teacher conferences. Kevin came to my classroom to visit about Jonah. I could tell he was exhausted and frustrated, and I knew he had every right to be. I explained to him that I knew Jonah was fighting him on everything he did. Kevin confided that Jonah loved Trisha and tried hard to do what she asked, but everything he did and every time he got involved with Jonah, it was horrible. He honestly didn't know if he could continue. He said they had tried counseling, but that it was a continual fight every day, every minute. He really was distraught.

I listened carefully to Kevin. I could see the pain and hurt in his eyes. I knew he was really trying but was at his wit's end. We sat in silence for a minute. At first, I didn't know what to say, but then, as if someone else was speaking through me, I sat up straight and looked him in the eye and said, "You can't give up on him. He is testing you because he believes he is a throwaway kid. He knows his mom threw him away, and he knows his dad threw him away. He doesn't trust men because they were supposed to have been taking care of him, but they haven't. He believes he is the grown-up and that his job is to take care of Peggy. You have stolen his job, and if he has any inkling that you're going to give up on him and throw him away, you will be just like all the other men in his life."

Kevin was listening intently as I continued. "You guys are at a crossroads in Jonah's life. You have the chance to teach him to be a good man, a kind man, a responsible man like you are, but if you give up on him, I promise he will become the man his father is. You are his greatest chance. I care so much about that little boy, and so does Trisha, but you're the most important person in his life right now. Your decision will determine the kind of man that boy grows up to be!"

Kevin had tears in his eyes when I finished. I knew I had overstepped my bounds. Holy cow, I was just the teacher and had no right to be so forceful, but I couldn't help myself. Silence surrounded us. I wiped away my tears. Kevin shook his head and stood up. He stuck out his hand to shake mine.

He said, "Thank you for your time," and walked out of the room.

Wowzers, I was shaken. I had no idea where that speech came from. I think Kevin could have gone to the principal and the school board and filed a complaint because of the things I had said to him, but he didn't. He was very gracious. He didn't say anything. I prayed that I had not made things worse. I was concerned. I think he realized that I didn't want him to give up on Jonah. I was well aware that I had laid a lot of responsibility at Kevin's feet, but I knew in my heart that he was a good man, and I hoped for the best.

As the year went on, Jonah seemed to get happier every day. He was bright and insatiable when it came to learning. He told me that Trisha helped him with his reading, but Kevin helped him with his math. I was thrilled. He told me that Kevin was really smart when it came to math, so he was going to be really smart, too.

At the end of the school year, I knew I had to say goodbye to my little friend Jonah. He promised he would come and see me when he was a third grader. My heart hurt because I knew I was going to miss him so much. I loved this little family they had created of Kevin, Trisha, Jonah, and Peggy. I gave them a gift certificate to go to our local dinner theater to see *Beauty and the Beast,* which would be playing during the summer.

I worked at the theater in the summer, and one night, they all showed up. Peggy was wearing a princess dress, and Jonah was dressed in a suit. Kevin and Trisha were dressed in their finest Sunday clothes, as Jonah called them. Seeing them altogether brought a tear to my eye. They were so happy. While I was seating them, Trisha said, "We have a big surprise for you. Tell her, Jonah!" He was jumping up and down and said, "Guess what, guess what? Kevin and Trisha are going to adopt me and Peggy! They already filled out the papers and everything." Oh, my goodness, I was thrilled! They were all just beaming. They had a wonderful dinner and seemed to really enjoy the show.

During intermission, Jonah went to the restroom. When he

returned, he came up to me and asked, "Ms. Melanie, can I tell you a secret?"

"Of course you can," I said.

He whispered in my ear and told me that he and Kevin had made a deal. He said that they had agreed that, for a while, at least, Kevin would be the grown-up and Jonah could be the kid. Kevin said he would take care of Jonah and Peggy until he was ready to be a grown-up too. Jonah told me that he had never been able to be the kid before, and it was pretty fun. He said Kevin told him, "Jonah, you are no longer a throwaway kid! You are mine and Trisha's keep-forever kid."

Yup, I gave him a huge hug and had tears rolling down my face as I thanked him for being an amazing young man. As they left the theater that night, Trisha, Jonah, and Peggy all hugged me. Kevin shook my hand and tearfully whispered in my ear, "Thank you."

My heart nearly burst.

40

PEGGY

When I started teaching, I would say that about 75 percent of my class lived with their birth mom and dad. The trend has completely reversed. I have taught for 23 years so far, and I would estimate that about 25 percent of my students live with their original birth parents. Their little lives are filled with stepparents, grandparents, foster parents, aunts, and uncles. It's always interesting when I ask a child to tell me about their family. It's often a web of people coming and going in their lives and very confusing for a lot of kids.

Peggy was no exception. She was an adorable brown-eyed little girl with pixie-cut brown hair. I had previously taught her half-sister, Cammie, and her brother, Jonah. All three children had the same father. I knew the situation she had come from and was amazed at how healthy and happy this child was. Kevin and Trisha had adopted her and Jonah, and they were an amazing, happy family.

I loved listening to Peggy's stories about family outings and vacations and even the day-to-day tales of their lives. My heart warmed as she told about Jonah and Kevin building stuff together or playing games and having tons of fun as a family. I knew what this little family had been through up to this point and was overjoyed with the lives they now cherished.

One day at school, we were completing a project; we were writing autobiographies. We were having a discussion about writing a good, interesting topic sentence to introduce ourselves. I tried to explain that their sentences needed to include something that defined them. I gave a couple of examples.

If I were writing my autobiography, I would write: "Ms. Melanie always wanted to be a teacher and loves teaching children and loves music. She was born and raised in Idaho." Or "Justin (a child in our class) was born in Montana and loves sports and wants to grow up to be a cowboy. He lives with his mom and stepdad and has one brother." Or "Kara (another child in our class) has three sisters. She loves to dance and sing. She and her sisters are going to grow up to be famous singers and move to Hollywood."

The kids went to work on their autobiographies. They were adorable and heartwarming. Some of them were hilarious, and some were kind of sad, but my favorite was Peggy's because I knew her history.

This is what she wrote: "Peggy is a little second grader who used to have a really bad life. She has a real brother and a real dad, but her dad is sick, and they were all real sad because they can't live with him anymore. So, about six months ago, Peggy and her brother got adopted by fake parents, and they are the best real people she knows. And now they are all a real family, and now Peggy is real happy."

EPILOGUE

As I have reviewed the stories I chose to put in this book, I have laughed, and I have cried. I have relived wonderful memories and memories that hurt my heart. But mostly, I have been grateful for each little life that has touched mine in some way. There are hundreds more stories, hundreds more memories, hundreds more blessings that teaching has brought to my life.

There are so many life lessons I have learned from these precious little people. I've learned that children pay attention to everything their parents teach them. They copy, they parrot, they repeat, and they believe in everything they see and hear. They are created in their home environment and need to fit into a classroom environment. What happens at home matters so much, and we teachers are eager to partner with parents to ensure that both the home and the school environment serve the children.

Parents matter to kids. Moms are vital to every child. Good moms are a blessing. Dads matter. Good dads are magical. Families are great. Good families are miracles. A child's sense of self begins in a consistent, reliable, caring, healthy home. Nothing can compensate for failure in the home. A teacher's most important job is to help good parents raise good, educated people.

I also learned that kids can tell when you like them and especially when you don't. They can read your feelings and body language like a book. I truly believe that kids do not care how much you know until they know if you care. Every minute you spend building a relationship with a child will show in their ability to learn and care about learning.

Happy kids make good, joyful learners. Kids like to be active and move around a lot. Bad behavior usually comes from great pain or undetermined anger. It's so important to realize that the hardest children to love are the children who need your love and care the most.

I know I have had the great privilege of being the teacher of several special starfish. I think about them and say a silent prayer that, in some way, I have had a positive influence in their lives.

Each fall, as I prepare for a new school year, I am excited to meet each new little child, each new little puzzle, each new little person who could grow up and change the world. I thank God for the opportunity I have had to get to know each little one — each little starfish. I pray that God will help me be what each little one needs, be it God, or Allah, or Jehovah, or Yahweh, or Brahman, or Vishnu, or Krishna, or the Tao.

Personally, I believe with all my heart that a higher power looks out for these kids. I know that I can be the hands that God needs to wipe away their tears, the arms He needs to hold them and let them know they matter, and the heart to show them that someone cares because I know that God loves them so much. I believe He wants us to save each little starfish, so I know with all my heart that he wants us to do everything we can to help each little precious child.

Over the years, due to some very bad teachers, we are no longer allowed to touch children. We cannot rub their backs or hold them in our laps or give them much-needed hugs. It's a tragic loss for lonely children who need a loving touch from a caring teacher who they have learned to trust. Shame on those bad, cruel teachers.

I count my blessings every day for the children put in my care. Some will be well cared for at home, and some will be from broken homes. Some will be hopelessly poor, and some will feel safe. Some will be scared, and some will be angry. Some will be happy, and some will be broken. But they all will be children who need someone to care about them, to listen to their needs, and to lift them up. I can teach them to love to learn, and I can teach them to care about others, but mostly, I can teach them that they matter — that every single one of them matters.

Teaching is the hardest, most exhausting, sometimes painful, heart-breaking, but most fulfilling career you can ever choose. It's a calling, and it's not for the weak or puny or selfish. As I walk along the beach of life and see each little childlike starfish fighting for a chance to survive, for a chance to learn, for a chance to thrive, I am so grateful that I can be their caregiver, their mentor, their friend, their cheerleader, their coach, their confidant, their hand-holder. But mostly, I am so grateful every day that I have been chosen to be their teacher. I realize I can't save every small soul, but those who have touched my life, I love dearly. Oh, I do hope that others, who will lovingly reach out to the starfish in their care, will answer the call. God bless each precious little child, each precious starfish.

PART III

ADVICE FOR TEACHERS AND PARENTS

Have you heard the phrase, "I wish I knew then what I know now"? That is how I feel about teaching. I am completing my 23rd year and have learned from my experiences so many amazing, helpful teaching ideas that I feel make me a better, more caring teacher. I wish I had learned them earlier in my career and thought I might share them now with anyone who is interested.

ALL TEACHERS HAVE TWO BALLS

Some of the best advice I ever received was from one of my favorite principals. She had been a remarkable teacher and was an incredible principal. She had been in the trenches with us. Those were the words she used to describe how challenging it is to be a good teacher. She worked tirelessly to help us improve our teaching and have pride in our school.

I have had ten principals in my 23 years of teaching, and I have enjoyed and learned from every one of them. This principal in particular was a spitfire of a person. She was a tiny lady with a ton of energy and spunk. She made up school cheers for the kids to repeat at our school and had fun assemblies and programs to let the kids know that we cared about them and their lives and their learning. My dad would have called her a little whipper-snapper because she had a contagious energy and an excitement for life and education.

The first time she spoke to us as a staff, she gave a remarkable speech. I had been teaching for about 15 years at this point, and wished I had heard the speech earlier in my life. She shocked us by announcing to the whole faculty that "all teachers have two balls!"

We all looked at the two embarrassed male teachers in the room. Their faces went bright red, and then everyone started to laugh. To avoid a sexual harassment charge, she quickly went on to explain her statement. "You need to think of your life as if you're holding two balls. The first one is made of precious, irreplaceable crystal. It's delicate and fragile and can never be replaced. If you drop it, the beautiful crystal ball will shatter and can never ever be repaired or replaced.

"The second ball is a remarkable ball made of metal covered with solid gold. It's of much worth. It's valuable and can provide you a wonderful, fulfilling life. You have worked hard to receive this amazing gold-covered ball and work hard to keep it shiny and in tip-top shape, but if you ever drop it, the golden ball will not shatter. Someone else can pick it up and carry it for you, and you can retrieve it later when you're ready to handle it again. It cannot shatter."

She went on to explain that these two balls represented your life. The crystal ball represents your family, your children, your significant other, and the life you have built for yourself outside of school. Don't drop that ball because you can never put it back together again. It will change with time, but it's more precious than anything else in your life. Your children will grow up and move on, but if you drop that precious crystal ball, you can never go back and save it.

The gold-covered ball is your job. It's of great value and worth. You keep it shined and brilliant. You work hard to increase its value, but if you should happen to drop it or let it slip, someone else can pick it up and carry it for you for a while or help you shine it again when you're ready. Don't let the golden ball crush the crystal ball. If you can't carry them at the same time and you must choose, let someone else help you with the golden ball. If you can only carry one, let it be the crystal ball.

I was so struck by her speech. I knew there were several times in my career that I had let the crystal ball become damaged. I had missed too many field trips with my own children or games or performances they had been involved in. They both turned out to be remarkable adults and amazing people, but I missed things in their lives I shouldn't have because I was too busy carrying that golden ball. I know it's a juggling act, but please make sure your own personal relationships don't suffer because you want to be a gold medalist.

MONEY MATTERS IN A TOKEN ECONOMY

In my classroom, we have a "token economy." It works wonderfully because it teaches the kids if they work hard there is a reward that teaches a life lesson. I pay the kids classroom money for different things. The money consists of gray paper quarters and green dollar bills. For example, they can earn $3.00 for completing and returning their homework. They get paid for looking up words in the dictionary or writing a paper that needs no editing.

They get paid for working hard and showing improvement or completing a challenging assignment. I explain that, in the real world, people get paid for working hard and improving. I pay them for 100% on their A.R. reading book tests because it means they have read it carefully and comprehended what they read.

They have piggy banks hanging on the front of their desks. They put their money in there, and once a month, we have a class store. They can spend their money on actual items that they get to keep. I budget about $25.00 a month of my own money to stock the store. I investigate what the kids are interested in and purchase those things. I have bought many Pokémon cards, bubbles, balloons, bracelets, seashells, small stuffed animals, bouncy balls, etc.

One of my favorite parts about our token economy is that it

takes a lot of arguing out of the classroom discipline. I charge the kids for things that I have explained before so they can't argue about it. A perfect example is not writing their names on their papers. They can pay me a dollar or do the assignment again. They always choose to pay a dollar and usually write their names on their papers after that. Or, for safety reasons, I charge them 25 cents if they don't push their chairs under their desks so the other kids don't trip on them. I charge them for blurting out answers to questions before the other kids have had a chance to figure out the answer.

It's hard for the kids to argue when they know the rules.

TATTLING VS. PROBLEM-SOLVING (THE GREAT DEBATE)

My favorite and most useful charge in our token economy is a charge for tattling. I teach them to problem-solve before they can tattle. If they don't try to solve the problem first, I charge them 50 cents per tattle. I teach them the difference between tattling and reporting. Reporting usually includes someone bleeding or explaining what they saw happened to someone else. I believe that 99% of all the issues that kids tattle about can be solved if they would talk to each other. If a child comes to me and says, "Johnny crowded" or "Jill hit me," my answer is always "It sounds like you have a problem to solve. Would you like to pay me to help, or would you like to try to solve it?" If they try and it fails, I will help, but they must at least try.

Almost every time, when the child goes back to solve the problem, the other child will say the behavior was either an accident or the other child did it first. It's an amazing thing to watch. I usually stay close to the discussion to make sure it's not a serious problem, but they almost always work it out.

The other thing that is amazing about problem-solving is that it's very empowering to the child. I explain that tattling makes them a victim and that we have no victims in our class. We only have teammates and friends. We work things out. We talk things over, and that makes us a stronger, better, more understanding team. They know that every teammate matters.

The key to problem-solving is the use of "I feel" statements. I use finger puppets to demonstrate the process at the beginning of the year. It goes like this:

"Stop, I have a problem with you [pushing me, cutting in line, etc.] It makes me feel ([frustrated, angry, hurt, mad, etc.] Let's talk about it please!"

I teach the kids that when someone says that to them, they are to stop, listen, and solve even if they didn't know there was a problem. It's almost always an accident or they were trying to get the other child's attention. It really works miracles.

I have had several parents contact me and ask, "What is this 'problem-solving' thing all about? My child is doing it with their siblings, and it's amazing!" I explain it to them, and they try it at home. Almost all kids would rather problem-solve than pay.

THE HIGHER LAW OR THE GOLDEN RULE

On my classroom ceiling, I have a poster that reads "Treat Others the Way You Want to Be Treated." I explain to the kids on the first day of school that that saying is our class motto and our higher law. All things that happen in our class go back to that rule. I tell them it's also called the "Golden Rule." We all lie on the floor and look at and read the rule over and over again. I ask the kids, "How do you want to be treated? Do you want me and the other kids in the class to listen to you when you talk? Do you want to be able to solve problems? Do you want to be able to learn in a happy, friendly environment? How do you want our classroom to be? Do you want people to treat you kindly and with respect? What do you want here?"

When a child is having a hard time listening to instructions or blurting out answers during a lesson or interrupting others, I ask them to go study our "higher law." They go and lie down on the floor, read, the rule over and over again and then return to the group with a thumbs up, saying, "I am ready to listen and be respectful." They are always welcomed back and thanked for following the Golden Rule.

On Constitution Day, the kids vote on what to put in our Classroom Constitution. Constitution Day happens in November. By then, they know and understand the value of the Golden Rule and vote to have that be our official Constitution. We write it out, and all the kids sign it with a feather pen just like the signers of the actual Constitution did. It's really an amazing process and cements them as part of our team. We hang our signed Constitution on our wall for the rest of the year.

SHARING CIRCLE FUN

Our school counselor introduced Sharing Circles to us several years ago. There is no better way to build team spirit in your classroom. I remind the kids about the higher law and that they need to listen and respect each other during the Sharing Circle.

We gather on the floor and sit in a large circle. I make sure everyone has a place and is comfortable. We have a microphone and show the kids how to use it. They pass it around when it's their turn to talk. I usually start by saying, "Good morning, my name is Miss Melanie."

In unison, the kids say, "Good morning, Miss Melanie." I will then explain what we are talking about that day in Sharing Circle. It can include how their weekend was or how they are feeling that day. I have asked kids to tell us about their favorite food, something they are worried about, a time when they were mad, or something that makes them happy. The key is to make sure they are listening to each other.

Pass the microphone around and have each child introduces themselves. Everyone responds, "Good morning, (we all say the child's name)." Then the child answers the question. I teach the kids to look at and smile at the person talking. We talk about respect and about how important it is to look at someone when they are talking to you. They tell me it feels good when people care about what they have to say. They feel welcome and part of the team.

I always make sure to notice children who are absent and comment on how sad I am and that they are missed. I am very cognizant to make sure I welcome them back when they return.

I am continually amazed at how children will bond with each other during a Sharing Circle. If one child had a bad experience or something bad happened to them, there is always someone in the group who has had a similar thing happen to them and will empathize with their situation.

It's remarkable to listen to the kids' different reactions to the same situations that we experience as a class. It's the best way to build empathy in children when they can actually see and hear how their peers are feeling. We need to teach their HQ (heart quotient) as well as their IQ (intelligence quotient).

After the Sharing Circle, everyone stands up in a tight circle, and we do a class cheer to start the day: "Go, go, go Team Miss Melanie. Yeah!!!!"

SHOW-AND-TELL TIME

Over the years, I have learned that there are two schools of thought on Show-and-Tell. Some people think it becomes a bragging contest, and some people think it's really good for kids to get up and talk to their peers about something that is important to them. I agree with both schools of thought.

At the beginning of the year, I communicate with the parents about Show-and-Tell and explain to them that their child needs their help. They are not allowed to bring toys or electronics to show. I explain that, once a week, their child gets to bring something educational to share with the other students. If they forget on their assigned day, they wait until the next week. I have five children share per day, and it only takes about ten minutes.

It's fascinating to see what parents send and how interested their child is in the artifact. It helps us get to know each little one and learn about what is important to them.

Many kids bring things from their vacations, some bring things their grandparents have sent. The child must be able to identify what educational area the items are related to. Is it math, science, social studies, art, reading? Some parents write a note for the child to read as they share something from their childhood. One child brought his aunt and uncle that live in China to show us how to use chopsticks. One little girl's dad came in once a week for six weeks to show us things he'd gotten in Russia. Another child had his brother, who was playing football at the local university, bring in his uniform and pads, and one little girl's mother came in and showed us her Army fatigues and let us lift her body armor. One little boy and his dad did a science experiment each week, and he would bring it in and tell us about it.

Some kids brought in cool rocks they had found, and others brought impressive leaves or pinecones. They explained the part these items play in nature. One little girl brought in her baby clothes that now fit her doll because she was a preemie. One child showed a cow his grandpa had whittled from wood. One child brought in a playbill from a local production of *Joseph and the Amazing Technicolor Dreamcoat* and taught us how you act at a live theater show. Kids showed talents they had been working on including a song on the piano, dance steps, karate moves, or the performance of a song they had written. The key was that they had to plan it before they came to school.

With parental help, Show-and-Tell can be a magnificent, educational experience for all concerned.

COMMUNICATION WITH PARENTS

Over the years, I have found that most parents want to help their child's teacher educate their child successfully. I work hard to communicate with parents. I have a class blog (called missmelaniesmunchkins.blogspot.com), and I send home notes and calendars at least once a month and make many phone calls.

I update my classroom blog about once a week. It shows pictures of their kids and what activities and projects we do in our class. Parents thank me continually for posting because they love to talk to their kids about the things we are learning in class, and the kids love to see their little faces on the computers and love to talk about what they are learning.

One of the most valuable things I do is give parents a list of questions to ask their child, which encourages them to discuss what happened at school that day. I explain that they should never ask a question that can have a one-word answer like "How was school today?" The answer will always be "fine." Personalize it for your classroom. I do often send home a particular note that says, "Have your child teach you about [have your child include a specific thing they have learned]. If they do and the parent signs it and returns it to school, the child will receive a classroom dollar.

CONVERSATION STARTERS

17 PROMPTS TO GET A CONVERSATION STARTED WITH YOUR KID(S)

Here is an example of a list I share with parents.

1. Tell me three things your teacher said today.
2. Tell me about something your teacher read to you today.
3. What was the main idea of a story your teacher read today? Who were the characters? What was the setting? What was the plot? Tell me the beginning, middle and end of the story.
4. Teach me two strategies you've learned to add or subtract or count or add money or numbers together including math mountains, expanded notation, regrouping, proof drawings, etc.
5. What do you know about writing a complete sentence? What does C.U.P.S.S. mean? (Capitalization, Understanding, Punctuation and Spaces, and Spelling)
6. Who did you play with at recess and what did you do?
7. How do you make sure that everyone has a friend at recess?
8. What did you talk about in Sharing Circle today?
9. What was one thing someone shared at Show-and-Tell?

10. What was something that challenged your brain today?
11. Tell me about the characters or setting of the book you read today?
12. Can you count by 2s, 5s, 10s, and 25s to 100?
13. Tell me your address, phone number, parents, and grandparents names.
14. What is your plan to correctly spell your spelling words this week?
15. What is your plan to complete your homework this week?
16. What are four of the rules that you follow at your school?
17. Teach me a song your teacher taught you or sang with you today.

FINAL THOUGHTS

Dear Parents,

Every teacher is grateful that you share your child with them. Please know how much they care for your little ones. Teachers know that it takes a village to raise a child into a happy, healthy, well-adjusted adult.

Please know how much your child's teacher wants to be part of that village. When a teacher reaches out, please be willing to reach back. We truly want what is best for your child.

Working together, parents and teachers can save every single starfish.

With love and care,

Melanie Parrish Anderson

Melanie Parrish Anderson began her teaching career 23 years ago in kindergarten and Title One Math. After seven years, she transferred to second grade where she has been ever since. Miss Melanie graduated from Idaho State University with a B.S. in Elementary Education and a B.A. in Early Childhood Education. She is the mother of two amazing children, the step-mom of two awesome sons, and the bonus-mom of five delightful people. She adores all 16 of her grandchildren. She is happily married to a wonderful man named Kevin. Melanie is so excited to finally finish her book. The book may be complete, but her teaching adventure continues.

You can contact the author at **allstarfishmatter@gmail.com**.

For more information about this book, please visit **www.MelanieParrishAnderson.com.**

MORE LESSONS LEARNED

Are you a teacher, administrator, counselor, or support staff with your own stories to tell? Happy, sad, frustrating, or heartfelt — we would love to hear them!

Please visit **www.MelanieParrishAnderson.com** to share your stories with us.

Teachers truly are a special gift. Thank you for all that you do to help the starfish in your life. You really do make a difference.

Made in the USA
San Bernardino, CA
23 February 2018